Garden Graphics

HOW TO PLAN AND MAP YOUR GARDEN

Gemma Nesbitt

Capability's Books

Deer Park, WI 54007

To Anna and Matthew

Originally published in Great Britain by Viking 1993

Copyright © Gemma Nesbitt, 1993
All rights reserved

Printed in Great Britain by Butler & Tanner Ltd, Frome and London

Published in the United States in 1993 by
Capability's Books, Inc.
2379 Highway 46
Deer Park, Wisconsin 54007

ISBN: 0–913–643114

Library of Congress Catalog Card Number: 93–71497
10 9 8 7 6 5 4 3 2 1

First U.S. Edition

'Capability's Books' and colophon are trademarks
of Capability's Books, Inc.

Contents

Acknowledgements

I would have been unable to write this book without the generous help of Kirsty Fergusson, head gardener at Mapperton House, Dorset, and her considerable knowledge of plants and gardening. Kirsty has written the great majority of the accompanying texts in the garden photograph section, and has also compiled the list of garden plants and vegetables in the dictionary of graphic symbols. My agent, Caroline Davidson, has given me a good mix of detailed advice and friendly pressure. Eleo Gordon, my editor, has been a fount of infectious enthusiasm throughout, and Annie Lee and Dinah Benson have provided meticulous help as my copy-editor and designer. My father, Michael Culme-Seymour, has buoyantly supported me. I also thank Antony Martin for his consistent encouragement.

At various stages of working on this book I have had good cause to thank the following gardening experts: Barry Ambrose of the Royal Horticultural Society; Elizabeth Banks, Elizabeth Banks Associates Ltd, London; Brian Davis, author; Daphne Dormer, The Chelsea Gardener, London; Brendan Lehane; Georgina Livingstone, landscape architect, London; the National Gardens Scheme (NGS) Secretaries of Scotland, Kent and Gloucestershire; Roger Phillips; Malcolm Shennan, garden designer, of Yeovil, Somerset; Stephen Slade, Hillier's Nurseries, Hampshire; Michael Wallis, Scott's Nurseries, Merriott, Somerset; and Sarah Wood of Wood Giangrande Landscape Gardeners, London.

The gardeners and owners of the gardens I have photographed have been very kind in helping me to identify the plants in their borders, thus enabling me to make accurate maps. I give addresses only for professional garden designers and those gardens/nurseries open to the public on a regular basis. They include: Ken Akers Garden Design, Saling Hall Lodge, Braintree, Essex (p. 28); Resi Andrups; Terry Baker; Tim and Bob Bartlett; Sarah Baldwin of the National Trust, Castle Drogo, Devon (p. 24); Peter Bedford; Veronica Cecil; Mrs Gerald Coke, Jenkyn Place, Bentley, Hampshire (p. 26); Nicola Cox; Jan Edge; Alice Fishburn; Wendy Francis, The Anchorage, 8 Croydon Road, West Wickham, Kent (p. 32, garden open through the NGS); Perceval Hayman; Joanna Hines; John and Caryl Hubbard; Mary Keen; Georgia Langton and Mrs Taylor Smith; Christopher Lloyd; Mr D.S. Moore, caretaker of the Turner Marina moorings, Little Venice, London; Patrick Niven; Alex Pankhurst, author of *Who Does Your Garden Grow?*; Elizabeth Parker-Jervis; Wendy and Michael Perry, Boswigo House, Truro, Cornwall (p. 36); Lady Anne Rasch, Heale, Middle Woodford, Wiltshire (p. 40, garden open all year); Serena Remnant; The Marchioness of Salisbury, Hatfield House, Hertfordshire (p. 64, gardens open from late March to mid October); Mr C.J. Skinner of Leeds Castle Enterprises, Kent (p. 67); and Douglas Strachan.

Introduction

Gardening, for most of the people who do it, is either heavy work or a beloved pastime. But it is an art form too – a 'people's art'. Unlike a painting, a garden is not fixed for all time. It is more like performance art, and gardeners have always wanted to keep records to capture the fleeting moment in what they have created. Before the present day, with its studious interest in garden history, garden designers paid little attention to the genius of their predecessors. 'Capability' Brown and others simply hired the eighteenth-century equivalent of a bulldozer and refashioned the landscape without a qualm. Michelangelo would never have overpainted a Leonardo so ruthlessly.

The art of making gardens is a conservative one, for conventions in design move slowly and fashions for particular plants or colour schemes have a long innings. Gardens themselves are ephemeral and perpetually in transition. A garden looks different between June and July – one plant dies back, another takes over. But from one July to the next July almost everything will have changed, often subtly, but sometimes in a major way – for example, frost may have killed some plants, and others may have grown out of all recognition.

There are all sorts of ways of recording gardens. Writing about them is one of the most widely practised and accessible. Many gardeners wish they had 'the poet's feelings and the painter's eye', as was said of Lancelot Brown, who always encouraged his potential patrons by telling them that their land had 'capabilities of improvement' and thereby acquired his nickname. The Younger Pliny's descriptions of Italian gardens in the first century AD are all we have to help us imagine the garden of ancient times, but they both evoke the atmosphere and give detail as effectively as do many later plans.

Numerous painters have been inspired by gardens, from Poussin, Claude, Watteau, Monet and Miró to Michael Andrews and John Hubbard on the contemporary scene. A view can be idealized in a painting, but it can also be recorded faithfully and accurately. A painting is more personal than a photograph. What it cannot do is tell people precisely which plants they are seeing.

Photography is a younger technique of recording. It is quite hard to do well: garden photographers spend days getting up at dawn for that first light which doesn't materialize until lunchtime, when the sun suddenly comes out and all the colours reduce to a harsh sameness of tone. What the photograph gives is an image of one moment of one day in one year.

A garden map or plan has one great advantage over both painting and photography – the names of plants, their positions in relation to each other, and any changes in design can all be recorded. Victorian ladies with talent and little else to do did not scribble 'Larkspur' on their watercolours. Maps or plans also have their limitations. They are two-dimensional and gardens are three-dimensional. Plants will perhaps not grow as they should, or they may die, or they may far overshoot their expected size. A plan can only be a record of what was originally planted in the garden or of what was alive, well and normal in the year the plan was drawn. Last year I walked round a garden filled with rare and mature plants, the owners of which had commissioned a leaflet by a garden writer to describe what was growing where. The leaflet, although well and carefully written, did not enable me to identify at all readily the plants I was inspecting. I needed a map as well, to show me the exact positioning of trees, shrubs and other plants in relation to each other and to prominent landmarks such as a flight of steps or a stream. Without that, I was often unsure of just what I was looking at and whether I had found what had been described in the leaflet.

The aim of this book is to introduce a new and easy method of garden mapping that can be used for a variety of purposes. The idea has developed from the garden maps and graphic symbols for plants that I designed for *The Garden Border Book* by Mary Keen and myself (Viking, 1987). *Garden Graphics* is about making maps of gardens and not about gardening. My method of garden map-making differs from the conventional techniques used by professional designers. They often use overlapping circles and ovals of different sizes, with numbers inside which refer to an adjacent plant list. For border plantings the different plants are drawn as very rough shapes, with no effort to convey the visual character of the plant. Their objective is to convey to the client that the border will be fully planted and that when mature no earth will be visible. Usually, with that sort of plan, the only person who can visualize the future garden accurately is the person who drew it.

If professional garden plans pose problems for the experts, they are even more confusing for amateurs. My graphics are designed to give the layman an immediate idea of shapes, approximate sizes and relationships between the plants. I do not use the overlapping technique. My graphics show the spaces around the plants to enable approximately correct positioning at the planting stage, rather than the dense, overgrown impression given by professional designers.

First (p. 3) I take a brief look at the history of garden plans (maps), including examples of how professional garden designers and landscape architects make them today. Professional and keen amateur gardeners have usually kept some sort of record of what plants they have and roughly where they were originally put. Before the nineteenth century, garden plans included ornamental and extravagant designs of great artistic beauty in their own right. These were often pictorial plans of large-scale garden design, which did not name individual herbaceous plants in a border, or shrubs in a shrubbery, but gave the user a strong sense of the general appearance of the garden and often of the surrounding landscape as well. At the most modest level, records were simply lists of plant names with a number indicating how many plants of each kind were bought – or even just a bundle of receipts from the local nursery.

Next (p. 12) I explain how to make maps using the graphics. I describe how to adapt a graphic symbol to the map-maker's own needs in terms of size and shape, how to make a rough map, and how to take it through to a neat and highly detailed finished product, if that is what is wanted. I also offer various ways of using colour on maps to show what plants are in flower and what colours predominate at certain times of year, and suggest the materials most suitable for making finished maps.

The first main illustrated section of the book (p. 19) consists of twenty-nine chapters, each of which includes a photograph of a garden (or a portion of one), a map of the planting shown in the photograph (with a camera logo indicating the position from which the photograph was taken), a comprehensive plant list and a short description. The photographs have been chosen to show the widest potential for making maps. They include garden plantings that are formal and informal, urban and rural. They give examples of water in the garden, a rockery, a vegetable garden, a conservatory, a houseboat and arrangements of pots. The main point of these spreads is to show a range of map-making situations, for it is here that the use of the outline graphic symbols of garden plants is demonstrated.

These photographs and maps may have an interest for those readers who are not feeling inventive at the moment but want to create a new planting in their own garden. A reader who thinks one of the garden photographs worth copying can buy the plants listed, or similar ones, then take the map into the garden and plant roughly as I have drawn it. With any luck something like the photograph may emerge in a few years' time. Readers who use this approach should have some gardening experience, and should know about their climate and soil conditions as well as about the propagation, cultivation and growing habit of the plants suggested, as these matters fall outside the scope of the present book.

The heart of the book is its second main section: the dictionary (p. 83), which consists of some 950 graphic symbols of the most commonly grown garden plants in Britain, the United States and similar climates and cultures, together with 250 architectural devices and garden objects. In this reference section I have included trees, shrubs, climbers, perennials, alpines, annuals, water plants, ferns, ornamental grasses, herbs, vegetables, fruits and nuts, as well as garden buildings and objects such as sundials and sculpture, ways of dividing and surfacing gardens, water, topiary and mazes.

A Short Look at Historical Garden Maps

The English word 'garden' has the same root as the American 'yard'. Both mean an enclosure. Our word 'anthology', of Greek etymology, means a gathering or a collection of flowers. Gardens are thus anthologies in our flowery world of today. But flowers, as we shall see, have not always been an essential feature of gardens, which since Eden have satisfied many needs: as places of leisure, meeting places, welcoming places and sanctuaries. The ancient Greeks and Romans made town parks where they met and talked – the first Academy and Lyceum were born in their public gardens. Later they became sporting arenas for athletes, thereby fulfilling the Greeks' passions for intellectual and physical competition. These were the ancestors of our public parks.

The idea of a garden has evoked a rich variety of thoughts and interpretations over the years. Erasmus said that a garden should renew the spirit – a need which can apparently arise even when things in general are going well enough: a modern writer on garden design has suggested that 'If a man were in Heaven, he would wall off a portion and design it himself and call it Hell and go and sit in it from time to time just for relief.' Gardens are essentially places where nature is selected and controlled, leading some to see them as symbols of consciousness, as against

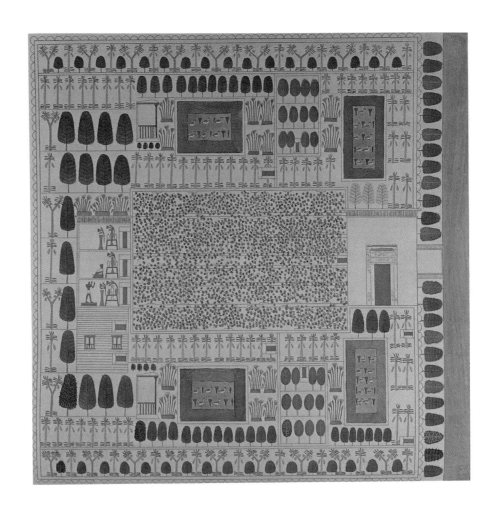

1. *Garden of a high court official of Amenhotep III at Thebes, c. 1400 BC.*

the wild forests outside the boundary which stand for the unconscious. Gardens have been compared to islands in an ocean. Then again they are feminine, because they contain: they are a precinct.

A very brief summary of how garden design developed will help to show how the map-making of a landscape has evolved into the

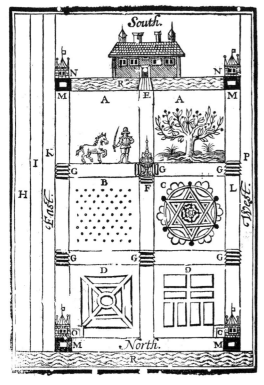

2. *Illustration from William Lawson,* A New Orchard and Garden, *1618. It shows a fountain (F), garden houses on mounts (M), and a knot design based on the rose of York and the six-pointed masonic star (C).*

more exact and detailed planting plans that are used today.

The illustration from ancient Egypt is, in essence, an architect's and irrigationist's planting and design plan [1]. The vines trained over pergolas in the centre, the trees, and the architectural features, such as the gate into the garden on the right, are shown in elevation (albeit facing in a funny direction), whereas the four ponds full of floating ducks are shown as bird's-eye views. This plan is closer to the method adopted in this book than maps of the intervening millennia, because of the combination of perspectives.

In Europe, garden plants and design emerged gradually. From the twelfth to the fourteenth centuries itinerant monks and crusaders returning home having seen Moorish gardens brought ideas which were developed in the monasteries and moated fortresses of the Middle Ages. Herbs were grown for medicinal and culinary purposes. From these came the Tudor knot garden. In illustration [2], the knot design is based on the rose and the star; a knot motif of interlaced snakes has been traced to Sumeria 5,000 years ago and has figured in many later cultures.

As the focus of life became more secular, the knot theme was incorporated into the geometric gardens of the seventeenth and eighteenth centuries. The confidence of the age was manifested and mirrored in its great gardens, which became a serious display of status. They showed the ideal dream world of their period. The famous design of 1728 by John James [3] is from the 'drawing-board garden' period. Its parterres contained few, if any, flowers; its 'points de vue' were, as the phrase implies, to be looked at from a distance.

Following designs like André Le Nôtre's for Versailles and Nicolas Fouquet's for Vaux-le-Vicomte, European styles of gardening crossed the Channel, brought by English landowners (in the main Royalists who had fled the Commonwealth). They came home to find their estates in disorder – trees and plants chopped down for fuel and fodder during their absence – and set about restoring them, partly in order to impress their authority on the unstable local rural workers. Two illustrations give an idea of the transition: an embroidered parterre, [4] and Eastbury [5]. Vast acreages of aristocratic estates were taken up; great parks and parterres stretching well beyond accurate human vision were laid out, and the results were recorded in exquisitely drawn pictorial plans, often done from an elevated viewpoint. In England all sorts of fantastic inventions from Renaissance models in Italy and France were imported to please and excite the grand landowner, who experimented with grottoes and hermitages, mazes and topiary, treillage and water tricks in his search for Utopia. Poets, men of literature, philosophers and architects frequently devised gardens for their patrons.

At different periods, the Belvedere in Rome, Versailles and Vaux-le-Vicomte outside Paris, and Stowe in Buckinghamshire each epitomized the vision of the epoch held by its patron and his designer. These visions are reflected in the magnificent way draughtsmen have portrayed their inventions in their maps. The picture-map [6] on p. 7 shows Stowe.

3. *John James's famous garden design of 1728.*

4. *'A parterre of imbroidery of a very new design'*
    from John James, The Theory and Practice of
    Gardening, *1728.*

Landscape garden and estate plans of this era cost a fortune to draw. The first garden plans were woodcuts; later they were done as engravings. Great books of plans on vellum, with added colour, were produced, but only the extremely rich could afford them. In those days it would not usually have been necessary to draw up detailed planting plans with named plants shown in relation to each other; the garden agent, a person of high stature on the estate, would have known which plants to plant where, told his under-gardeners to do it, and arranged it all.

In a fifty-acre garden and with the concept of a prospect uppermost in the minds of the designers, it was mainly distinguished specimen trees that were planted. In these noble centrespreads there were few flowers. On either side of the main vista there were usually more human-scale 'compartment' gardens, and in these little pleasure gardens flowers would have been planted in small beds of carefully weeded earth as single specimens – a peony, a lily or a rose. Or they might have been filled with bedding tulips to be followed by snapdragons. On the outside edges of the grand designs were walled gardens, some massed with flowers, others with vegetables, or used as orchards or small pretend wildernesses. The flowers would have a short season, a rose being in flower for perhaps just two weeks in the year. Throughout the ages of grand design, cottage gardens would have

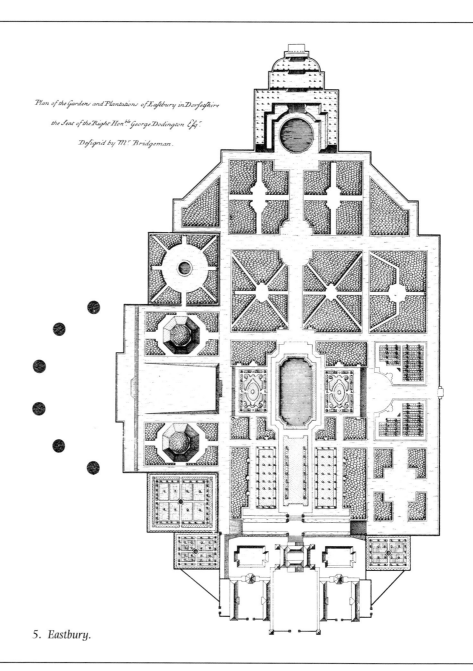

5. *Eastbury.*

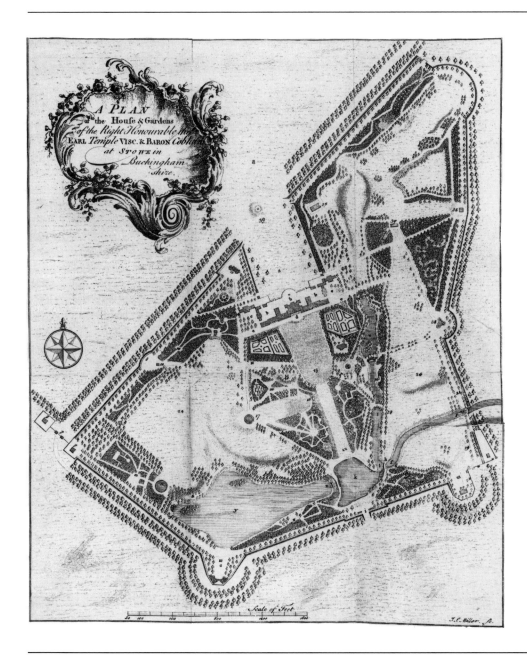

been places to supply produce, herbs and vegetables. They would also have had some early summer flowers. No records or made plans were kept of these.

Because of the Ice Age, indigenous plants were fairly limited in Britain. But ever since the Romans arrived, 2,000 years ago, travellers to all parts of the globe have brought foreign plants home with them. The process of serious plant-collecting has intensified ever since the medieval monk and crusader travellers. At first it was an academic pursuit and the plants were nurtured in botanic gardens, but the use of plants was also of great importance. In 1772 Joseph Banks took charge of the royal collection at Kew, which in that decade had about 5,500 plants: by 1813 this had doubled to 11,000, and by 1992 the number had nearly quadrupled again, to 40,000.

In eighteenth-century England the great formal gardens gave way to the landscape garden when 'Capability' Brown and Humphry Repton brought in Nature, with sweeping curves of fine trees and parkland. Geometry gave way to the wavy line. The 'genius of the place' – the character of the individual site – came to the fore. One reason for the change was that young gentlemen of the landowning class began doing the Grand Tour, and saw the classical landscape paintings of Poussin and other European painters

6. *Stowe: three designers worked here over a period. This shows the work after William Kent had finished (from B. Seeley,* Stowe, *London, 1769).*

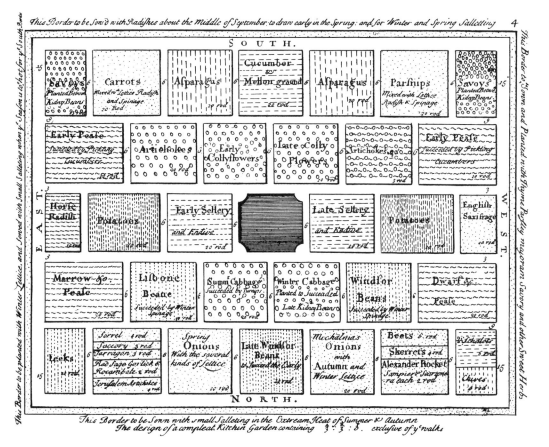

7. *From Batty Langley's* New Principles of Gardening, *1728, an early example of plant names being used in a plan.*

for the first time. Another cause was the prosperity that had come through a stable Whig government under the Hanoverian regime, which had enabled landowners to afford expensive landscaping and then to maintain their parks, which could be as big as 1,000 acres.

After the industrial revolution, a new type of smaller landowner emerged, one who had made his money from his industrial skills and wanted to build a house and make a garden, often near a town. Unlike the earlier aristocratic landowners who spent seasons in London and others in the country, he stayed at home all the year round. The Villa garden style, dating from the early nineteenth century, was one result. The estate and garden agents employed by these new landlords did not have the knowledge of those of previous generations; also, many more herbaceous perennials and flowering shrubs were available and interest grew in the shape and colour of leaves and flowers. Money and space were both in shorter supply, leading to smaller scale and denser planting schemes.

One of the many early landscape gardeners to draw maps for these new designs was J.C. Loudon; in 1836 he published a book with the telling title *Suburban Gardener and Villa Companion*. Illustrated here are two examples of border planting maps, one by Loudon [8] and the other by Gertrude Jekyll, about a century later [9]. Both plans are workmanlike and informative but not particularly pleasing as artworks: they do not give a sense of the 'architecture' of the border nor of the visual characteristics of any of the plants.

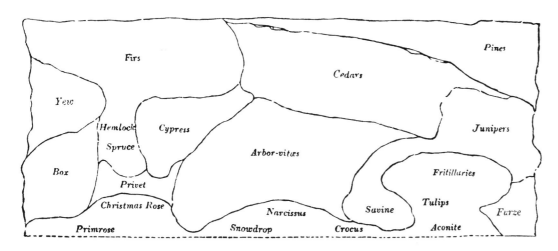

Gertrude Jekyll's plans show the relationship of plants inside the shape she has allowed, using a mixture of Latin and common names. Plans like hers have been used, with modifications, ever since. The following illustrations show the kinds of technique that are available to amateur garden designers today.

It is when it comes to professional landscape design that the amateur interpreter can feel baffled. On pp. 10–11 are various English and American contemporary methods of drawing plans. In [12], for a garden and a courtyard, it is anybody's guess whether the circular devices are parasols or trees; for the rest, the conventional manner of drawing the plans gives the reader information but little visual stimulus.

8. *From J.C. Loudon,* The Encyclopaedia of Gardening, *1827. This is one of the first plans of a modest-sized area which includes trees, shrubs and flowers.*

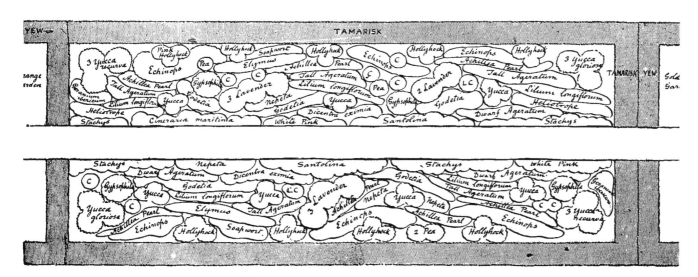

9. *Gertrude Jekyll's plan for a grey garden, from* Colour Schemes for the Flower Garden, *1912.*

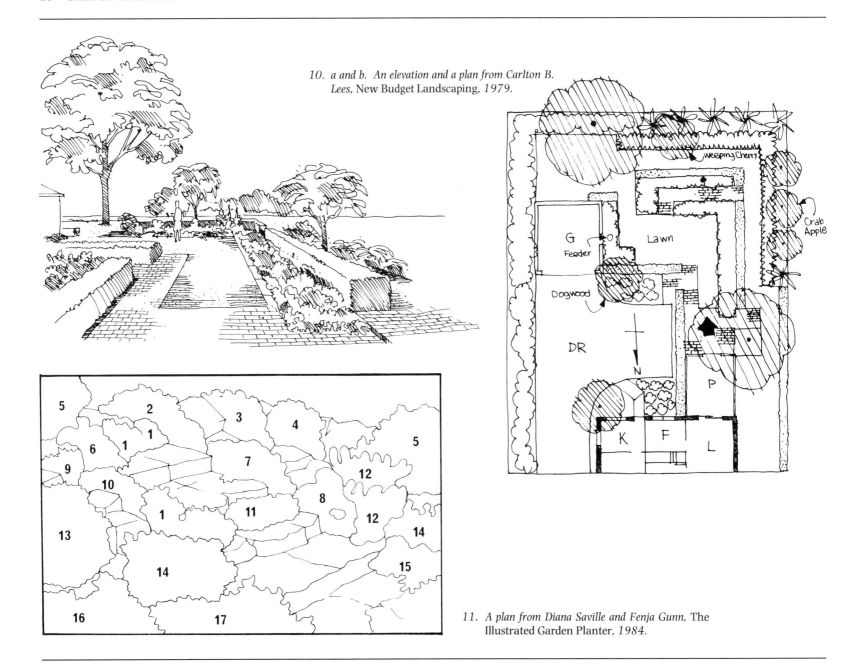

10. a and b. An elevation and a plan from Carlton B. Lees, New Budget Landscaping, *1979.*

11. A plan from Diana Saville and Fenja Gunn, The Illustrated Garden Planter, *1984.*

12. A contemporary American method of drawing plans.

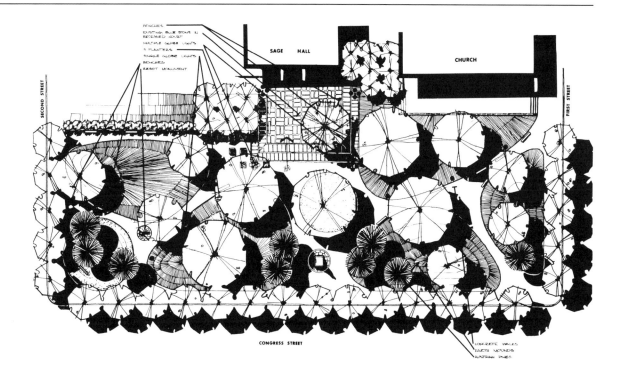

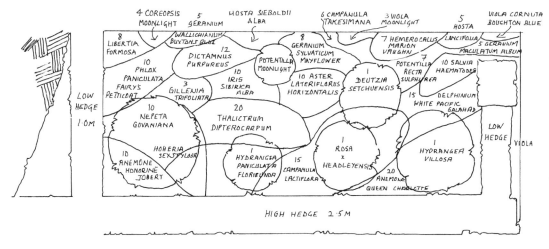

13. A detailed border planting plan by Elizabeth Banks and Associates Ltd for the Royal Horticultural Society garden at Rosemoor in Devon. It is intended for professionals but can also be read by amateur gardeners.

How to Use Garden Graphics to Make Garden Maps

This book can be used in two ways: for making a rough working drawing of an existing or yet-to-be-designed garden, or, more ambitiously, for making a frameable permanent record by carefully copying the symbols and using colour (see p. 14) and calligraphy. The plant symbols have been made as simple and easy to copy as possible, and drawing them bears no comparison with the fine art of botanical illustration – so do not be daunted.

You may not have considered spending time making a map of your garden, but it is a very useful record both for yourself as a gardener and for others who might want to copy a planting scheme or design in the future. Maps help communication between keen gardeners and can add a lot to the pleasure of people visiting gardens that are open to the public. Despite the labour involved, seasonal or even monthly maps showing the colours of plants in flower can be extremely rewarding. Rough scribbles can be done in the summer, and the detailed work kept for a dreary winter evening.

The 950 plant graphics in the dictionary (p. 83) represent some of the most common garden plants, specimen trees, popular weeds, edible herbs, vegetables, fruits and nuts grown in Britain and similar climates. There are so many varieties that no dictionary can

be fully comprehensive, but gardeners who want to use the graphics for making their own maps and cannot immediately find the plant symbol they need should be able to find a close relative by looking in a reference book to find a plant in the same botanical family and adapting the symbol slightly. For example, I have left out *Gazania* (treasure flower – a tender, half-hardy South African daisy-like annual). This belongs to the family *Compositae*, which also includes plants (such as *Dimorphotheca*, the Cape marigold or African daisy) for which symbols *are* to be found in the dictionary. *Crotalaria* (rattle-box, golden sweet pea), a half-hardy annual not included in the dictionary, belongs to *Labiatae*, the same family as *Lathyrus*, the common sweet pea. Again, this *is* in the dictionary and can be used as a model for *Crotalaria*.

The graphics given for architectural devices and garden objects may not correspond exactly to what readers have in their own gardens. Some of these graphics look complicated and may be less easy to copy than the plant symbols, but they can be adapted satisfactorily to a simple outline. There is no need to draw the thatch or tiles as I have for a summerhouse roof, for example. Equally, the time-consuming work I have done to make dots for earth or tiny circles for gravel can be omitted and those areas left blank.

In most of the plant graphics, the outline pattern is derived from one of the main visual characteristics in nature of that particular plant genus or species. The viewpoint is a layman's eye rather than that of the taxonomist or geneticist, and there is no botanical 'logic' to these symbols. The characteristics I have selected for different plants include leaf shape, petals, fruits, roots and overall shape. For coniferous trees I have used the general shape of the tree (height and spread of a mature specimen), while in the case of deciduous trees I have taken the leaf shape and used that. For fruit trees in the species *Prunus* and *Malus* I have followed the pattern I have used for other members of the same family, *Rosaceae*, and put a small, simple drawing of a pear, apple or cherry inside.

In the case of the large plant families – daisies (*Compositae*), peas and beans (*Leguminosae*) or mints (*Labiatae*), for example – I have given the member species a resemblance in the outline pattern of their graphic. But this cannot be fully consistent because I am aiming to give the visual character of a plant: for instance, *Compositae* is a huge family of common garden plants ranging from a 10ft (3m) high sunflower to a pincushion plant 3 inches (8cm) high. Within this family are members of the thistly *Carduus* tribe. So I have devised graphics with daisy-like petals for most *Compositae* annuals and perennials but a thistle-like outline for the *Carduus* tribe – *Onopordum*, knapweeds (*Centaurea*), *Cynara*, and *Echinops*.

Architectural plants – meaning those that stand out in an upright manner, ranging from trees and climbers to irises, ornamental grasses and ferns – are shown in elevation. Spreading, clumpy or bushy perennials and smaller shrubs are shown from a bird's-eye view point. Climbing, rambling or trailing plants mimic the shape of the area that the plant occupies.

In the dictionary all the symbols are much the same size, and when drawing your maps you will need to adjust the size to correspond with reality. You will need to know the size of the appropriate variety – maples, for example, range from tall and spreading trees to tiny ones like *Acer buergeranum* which are suitable for bonsai training. *Acer griseum*, with a maximum potential height of 15ft (5m), should be drawn smaller than *Acer platanoides*, which can reach a height of 40ft (12m). *Acer campestre* is used for pleaching and hedging and can be drawn accordingly (see the tree training and pleaching symbols on p. 178). There are even greater extremes: a *Sequoia* (Californian redwood) can grow to over 330ft (100m) and a *Senecio cineraria maritima* can be only 8 inches (20cm) high, but the *Sequoia* graphic in the dictionary is only two and a half times bigger than the *Senecio* graphic. The format of the book does not allow such extreme proportions of size to be demonstrated in the graphics, nor indeed could they be on any map the reader is likely to make. As it is unrealistic to draw to scale, you should

try to envisage the expected size of your taller plants and draw their symbols a bit bigger than the size drawn in the dictionary.

In the dictionary the plant graphics are listed alphabetically under their Latin names. Vegetables and soft fruits (listed by English name) and architectural devices and objects have their own sub-sections. The index includes botanical Latin and English common names. A name is written inside each plant graphic: this is the genus or species name of the plant. Map-makers should put in the name of their own variety/hybrid/cultivar if they want to record that amount of detail. To the right of each graphic is a short description. This includes the plant's genus or species name, its common name(s), its family, a brief description of what it is, its main flowering/colour feature, its main season and its average size, as in the following example:

Latin name	PARTHENOCISSUS
Common names	Virginia creeper, Boston ivy
Family	*Vitaceae*
Description, e.g. colour(s) and flowering season.	Deciduous self-clinging climbing shrub. Autumn colour.
Size: height/spread (in feet/metres).	Size: up to 70ft (20m). See var.

Where a species may have different varieties, I put 'See var.' in the colour, season and size information, meaning that readers should check their reference books to find out about their particular plant variety. In the text beside each graphic I have indicated the largest sizes each plant can be expected to achieve in Britain. I have described plants which usually grow to a height of 1ft (30cm)

as 'Very small', and those which reach about 2ft (60cm) as 'Small'.

If your aim is a neat final map, I suggest using a thicker pen when you draw the larger shrubs and trees. Shrubs have a short outline stem or trunk, and trees have a solid trunk. Since climbers, taller shrubs and trees are generally shown in elevation, they will stand out as realistically bigger than border, bedding and rockery plants.

Making a Map in Three Easy Stages

For your first rough design, go into the garden with paper and pencil and measure the planting scheme. You can use a tape-measure or just tread out the feet (yards or metres). On the following page I give a simple example.

1. The border measures 5 ft (1.5m) deep and 11 ft (3.3m) long and faces south. Roughly draw the shape in the correct proportions and put in a north-facing arrow. Show where any buildings and boundaries (walls, hedges, gates) are, and indicate permanent features like paved areas, steps, water, a lawn, the bigger trees, plant containers and so forth. In my example there is only a house wall and a paved terrace.

2. Next, draw in the positions of the main plants: trees, shrubs and perennials. Add details of underplanting, bulbs, annuals and any transient plants you want to record.

3. Once you are happy with the rough plan, go indoors and turn it into a finished map.

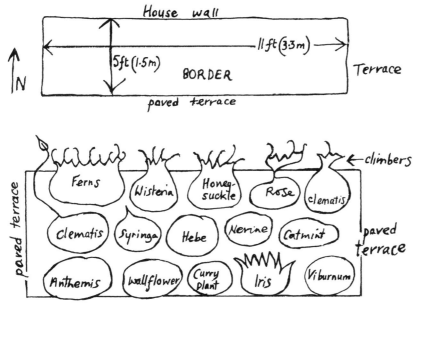

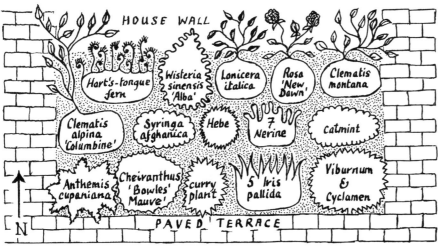

Check the graphic symbol for each plant in the dictionary section of this book, and copy it to a size appropriate for your planting. (Some people may prefer to make a tracing or a photocopy.) Then write in the plant's name in as much detail as you want to record. You can use common names for your plant graphics, though I have generally used the botanical Latin, this being the accepted international language.

To make the artwork for a permanent record, like those used in this book, I use Indian ink and a calligraphic nib on non-reproducing blue mm graph paper and, after cleaning it up, make a photocopy.

Your resulting garden map will resemble those I have drawn in the book's photographic and map section (p. 19). They will be a mixture of elevations and bird's-eye view graphics which show the position of each plant, its relation to its neighbours, and how much vertical and horizontal space it takes up. Its name will be written inside the symbol, with a number specifying how many plants of the same kind are used in any one clump.

Recording Colour in the Garden

There are several ways of recording colour in the garden, as shown in the following pages. Opposite I show four possible ways of recording the colours in the map on this page. There is a wide choice of media: coloured inks (neat and/or watered-down), watercolours, coloured pencils, felt-tips, children's wax crayons, pastels or chalks and spray-fix.

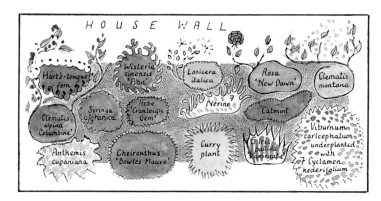

Photocopy your finished map and use watercolours to colour
in each plant. Mix your paints carefully to get as close as
possible to the plant's main colour.

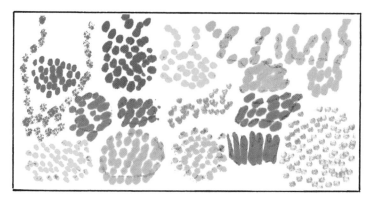

Felt-tips. These are easy to use but look rather crude unless
you stipple as here.

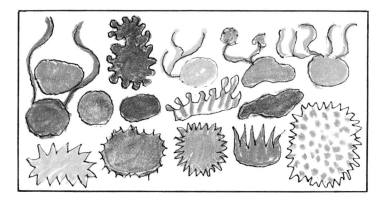

Redraw your map leaving out the plant names, and colour in
with coloured pencils.

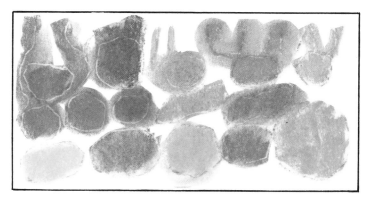

An impressionistic effect using pastels or chalks and a
finger-tip.

Mapping Seasonal Colour

Here is a black and white map of a small bed with a long flowering season. With it are five coloured maps which indicate in which months certain colours predominate. This way of recording colour gives a sense of full and mature plant growth, in contrast to the example on p. 14. In drawing these colour plans I have assumed that some or most plants overlap the months before and after the main flowering time: for example, in this planting the 'Bowles' Mauve' wallflower, rosemary, rose, *Clematis* 'Perle d'Azur' and romneya.

Having drawn your map, and unless your planting scheme is very much for one season only, make four or five reduced-size photocopies of it.

One is for early spring colour, one for mid to late spring, one for midsummer, one for late summer to early autumn and one for late autumn. If you just want an impression of the positions of the dominant colours, Tipp-Ex out those plants which are not in flower or not particularly impressive in any one season. Decide which plants flower when, and then colour in their outline symbols, using the tone closest to their natural hue in whichever medium you have chosen. The colours you choose may be flower, leaf or fruit colour or various greens. In this example of colouring I have decided not to use the outline graphic symbol of the black and white map but rather decided to do it a little more abstractly.

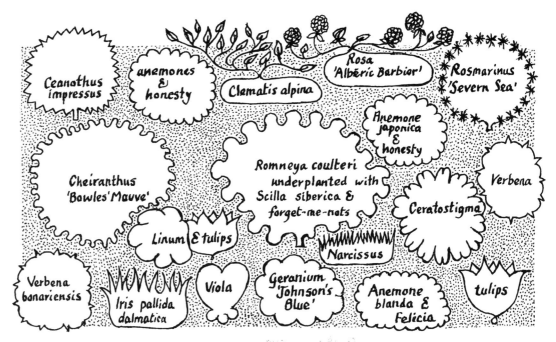

February/March

Cheiranthus 'Bowles' Mauve'
Scilla siberica
Anemone blanda

Rosmarinus 'Severn Sea'
Clematis alpina 'Frances Rivis'
Narcissus 'Thalia'

March/April

Rosmarinus 'Severn Sea'   *Ceanothus impressus*
Clematis alpina 'Frances Rivis'   *Tulipa* 'Queen of the Night'
Myosotis 'Blue Ball'   *Cheiranthus* 'Bowles' Mauve'

April/May

Iris pallida dalmatica   *Ceanothus impressus*
Geranium 'Johnson's Blue' *Viola* 'Huntercombe Purple'

June/July

Rosa 'Albéric Barbier'
Romneya coulteri
Clematis 'Perle d'Azur'
Felicia amelloides
Linum perenne

August/September

Aquilegia   *Rosa* 'Albéric Barbier'
Geranium 'Johnson's Blue'   *Romneya coulteri*
Anemone japonica   *Clematis* 'Perle d'Azur'
Verbena bonariensis   *Felicia amelloides*
Ceratostigma willmottianum   *Linum perenne*

Other Ways of Recording Colour

Here are two other ways of showing how a border changes colour at different times of year. The black and white map at the foot of the page shows everything planted. The three smaller ones above show three moments in the year, a shortish period from spring through June to July. In a simplified way these plans show the main flower colours but give no sense of density or abundance.

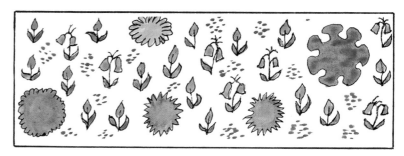

April/May   Crown imperials, daisies, forget-me-nots, peonies, sweet rocket, spiraea, tulips.

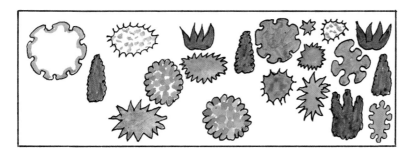

June   Crambe, gillenia, irises, lupins, peonies, poppies, sidalcea, sweet William, thalictrum.

July   Asters, baptisia, campanula, clematis, day lilies, morina, roses, sidalcea, verbascum.

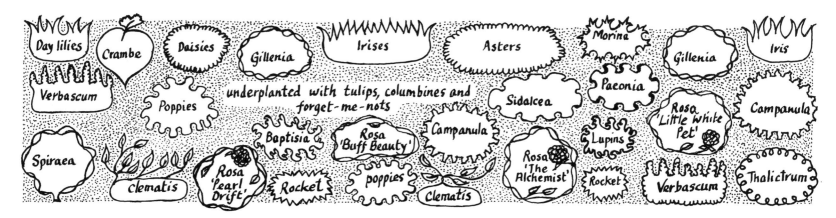

Designed Gardens

1 · A Rock Garden

Four high walls of mellow brick make this a warm and sheltered spot – a gardener's dream. The soil, however, is more of a gardener's nightmare: shallow and clay, it dries out quickly in the summer, 'locks up' nutrients and becomes sticky and heavy in the winter. Its owners have done much to improve the soil, but have wisely chosen plants which are adapted to dry conditions. From 1910 to 1930 this was a heath garden – which was not only very fashionable at the time, but well suited to the poor soil. An intricate network of paths threaded among little beds and rockeries, and the present owners simplified the complicated pattern by making two larger beds, separated by stone paths and centred around an old lichen-covered urn. By enriching the soil they have considerably extended the range of plants available to them, and they have also kept the maintenance low: one big clear-up in the autumn, and the garden seems to look after itself for the rest of the year.

Silver and grey plants, as a rule, do well in hot, dry positions: lavender, santolina, artemisia and anthemis are all clearly thriving here. White and yellow potentillas are also at home in these conditions; the red- and orange-flowered varieties tend to fade quickly in full sun. The rock rose (helianthemum) is another must for a warm, dry bank where it can spill over stony outcrops.

It is in the nature of plants adapted to poor, dry soils to cover the ground in low, mound-forming clusters, as this reduces the evaporation of moisture from the soil around the roots. Tall plants with anything more than needle-like foliage are not so easy to find in this situation; foxgloves and thalictrums, however, seem to manage in any kind of soil and make striking – if short-lived – upright accents among the silvery-green domes.

Plant list

Achillea 'Moonshine' (2)
Anthemis cupaniana
Artemisia absinthium 'Lambrook Silver'
Azalea (blue)
Chrysanthemum parthenium
Epimedium × rubrum
Fig tree
Foeniculum vulgare 'Purpurascens' (fennel)
Geranium 'Johnson's Blue' (2)
Helianthemum 'Wisley Primrose'
Hemerocallis
Lavandula spica (2)
Lupinus arboreus 'Golden Spire' (tree lupin)
Montbretia
Paeonia 'Duchesse de Nemours', P. 'Baroness
   Schroeder'
Potentilla fruticosa 'Katherine Dykes', P.f. 'Primrose
   Beauty'
Rosa rubrifolia (R. glauca)
Salvia officinalis 'Purpurascens'
Santolina incana
Sedum
Thalictrum
Victoria plum tree

Self-sown Digitalis purpurea alba (white foxgloves),
Linaria purpurea (toadflax)

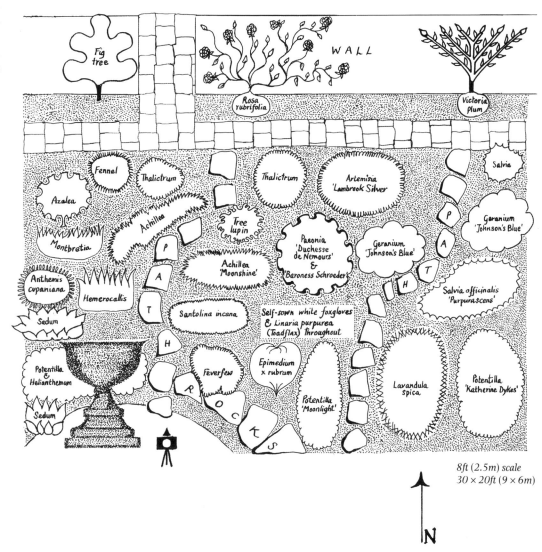

8ft (2.5m) scale
30 × 20ft (9 × 6m)

N

2 · A Bright Border

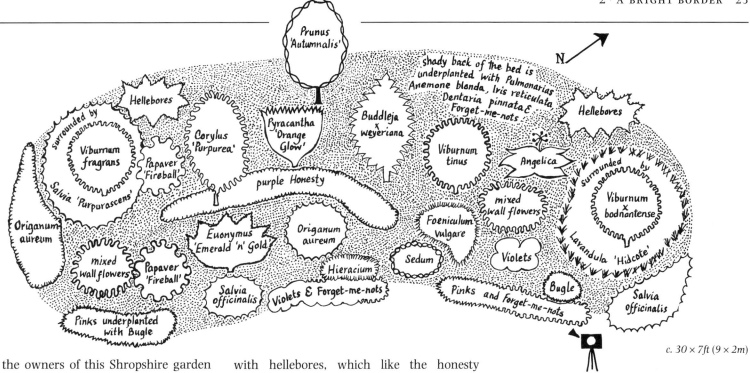

Prunus 'Autumnalis'

N

Helebores

surrounded by

Viburnum fragrans

Corylus 'Purpurea'

Papaver 'Fireball'

Pyracantha 'Orange Glow'

Buddleja x weyeriana

shady back of the bed is underplanted with Pulmonarias, Anemone blanda, Iris reticulata, Dentaria pinnata & Forget-me-nots.

Helebores

Salvia 'Purpurascens'

purple Honesty

Viburnum tinus

Angelica

surrounded by

Origanum aureum

Euonymus 'Emerald 'n' Gold'

Origanum aureum

Foeniculum vulgare

mixed wall flowers

Viburnum x bodnantense

mixed wall flowers

Papaver 'Fireball'

Hieracium

Sedum

Violets

Lavandula 'Hidcote'

Salvia officinalis

Violets & Forget-me-nots

Pinks and forget-me-nots

Bugle

Salvia officinalis

Pinks underplanted with Bugle

c. 30 × 7ft (9 × 2m)

When the owners of this Shropshire garden decided to turn a bank of holly bushes into a mixed border, their first concern was that it should be attractive to butterflies and bees. A border planted this way is fragrant and pretty from spring to late summer.

The garden is exposed, and all the plants have to be tough enough to cope with cold winds. The clay soil has been leavened with humus, and a little lime is added where the honesty and wallflowers are planted. The right-hand side of the border receives most of the sun; in the spring it is bright with wall-flowers, honesty and forget-me-nots, and these are succeeded by poppies, sweet scabious, marigolds, pinks and purple fennel. By September, the sedums and buddlejas are flowering. The shaded side on the left is filled with hellebores, which like the honesty and forget-me-nots self-seed, pulmonaria, *Dentaria pinnata* and *Anemone blanda*.

During the colder months, the border retains a structure of flowering shrubs. Late into autumn the orange berries of the pyracantha mingle with the copper tones of the corylus, which, in December, produces pale pink and mauve catkins. This is when the hellebores are flowering and they comple-ment each other well. The viburnums flower fragrantly through the coldest weather.

Plant list

Ajuga reptans 'Atropurpurea' (bugle) (3)
Angelica
Buddleja × weyeriana
Corylus 'Purpurea'

Euonymus 'Emerald 'n' Gold'
Foeniculum vulgare
Hellebores (3)
Hieracium
Lavandula 'Hidcote' (3)
Lunaria annua (honesty) (9)
Origanum aureum (5)
Papaver 'Fireball' (3)
Prunus 'Autumnalis'
Pyracantha 'Orange Glow'
Salvia officinalis 'Purpurascens' (3)
Sedum spectabile
Viburnum × bodnantense, V.fragrans, V.tinus
Wallflowers (mixed)

Underplanted with *Anemone blanda, Dentaria pinnata*, forget-me-nots, *Iris reticulata*, pinks, *Pulmonaria alba, P.longifolia, P.*'Munstead Blue', *P.saccharata, P.*'Sissinghurst White', violets

3 · Shrubbery Walk

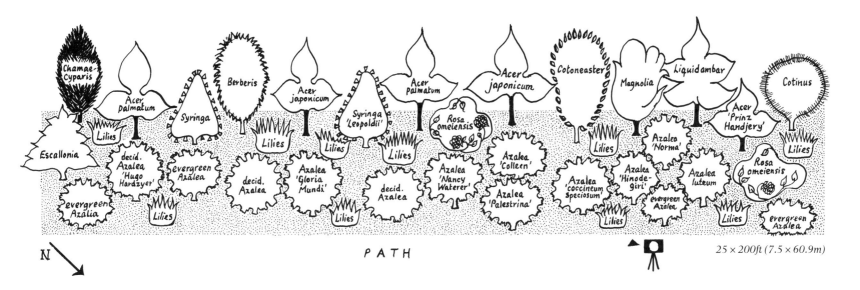

Chamae-
Cyparis

Acer
palmatum

Berberis

Syringa

Acer
japonicum

Acer
palmatum

Acer
japonicum

Cotoneaster

Magnolia

Liquidambar

Cotinus

Escallonia

Lilies

Syringa
'Leopoldii'

Rosa
omeiensis

Acer
'Prinz
Handjery'

Lilies

Lilies

decid.
Azalea
'Hugo
Hardzyer'

evergreen
Azalea

decid.
Azalea

Azalea
'Gloria
Mundi'

Lilies

Lilies

Azalea
'Nancy
Waterer'

Azalea
'Colleen'

Azalea
'coccineum
Speciosum'

Azalea
'Norma'

Azalea
'Hinode-
giri'

Azalea
luteum

Rosa
omeiensis

Lilies

evergreen
Azalea

decid.
Azalea

Azalea
'Palestrina'

Lilies

evergreen
Azalea

Lilies

evergreen
Azalea

Lilies

P A T H

N

25 × 200ft (7.5 × 60.9m)

This part of the garden at Castle Drogo in Devon is designed to look its best twice during the year: first in May and June, when the rich and colourful collection of azaleas are flowering, and again in the autumn, when the acers and liquidambar are aflame with crimson and gold. During the summer months, the many different varieties of lily provide a quieter interlude. A shelter-belt of holly, beech and pine trees has been planted to protect the border from the onslaught of the south-westerly winds, which can cause havoc in this part of the country.

Despite the splendid appearance, many of the shrubs from the original planting have died and a historically accurate replanting is to be started soon.

Plant list

Acer japonicum aureum (2), *A.palmatum atropurpureum* (2), *A.*'Prinz Handjery'
Berberis thunbergii
Chamaecyparis
Cotinus coggygria
Cotoneaster
Escallonia
Lilium 'Mrs R.O. Backhouse', *L.henryi*, *L.tigrinum*
Liquidambar
Magnolia 'Rustica Rubra'
Rhododendron (Azalea) 'Coccineum Speciosum',
    R.(A.)'Colleen', *R.(A.)*'Gloria Mundi',
    R.(A.)'Hinode-giri', *R.(A.)*'Nancy Waterer',
    R.(A.) 'Norma', *R.(A.)*'Palestrina', *R.(A.)luteum*,
    R.(A.)'Hugo Hardzyer'
Rosa omeiensis pteracantha
Syringa 'Leopoldii'

A high clipped yew hedge invites bold colours and shapes which will show up well against the dark green background. The large silvery cut leaves and striking thistle-like flowers of *Centaurea pulchra* 'Major' are a good response to this invitation. As these fade, the blue delphiniums and the golden daisy flowers of the buphthalmum will make a similar impact, and later still, when the faded delphinium spires have been cut down, the pink and orange lily-like blooms of the alstroemeria will stand out boldly against the wall of dark green. Alstroemerias look grand when they are flowering, but once they have finished, they look terrible. This is really the best place for them: at the back of the border, surrounded by lots of foliage and flowers which hide their messy demise. A gap has been left immediately in front of the hedge, for easier trimming and for access to the border, so that essential maintenance can be carried out.

The middle of the border and the foreground contain an uncompromising range of hot pinks, reds and mauves. *Geranium psilostemon* is worth growing for its foliage alone, which is deeply cut, brilliant green and coloured in the autumn. In June it is smothered in magenta flowers, each of which has a deep blue centre. Here, it is skirted with the pink and white dianthus 'Valerie Finnis' and the unusual *Diascia rigescens*. This, like its neighbour, *Penstemon* 'Firebird', is unlikely to survive harsh winters, so it is as well to take cuttings and overwinter them under glass.

Where there is only a shallow border beside a yew hedge, a simple planting of *Lychnis chalcedonica*, perhaps with *Verbascum bombyciferum*, looks very well.

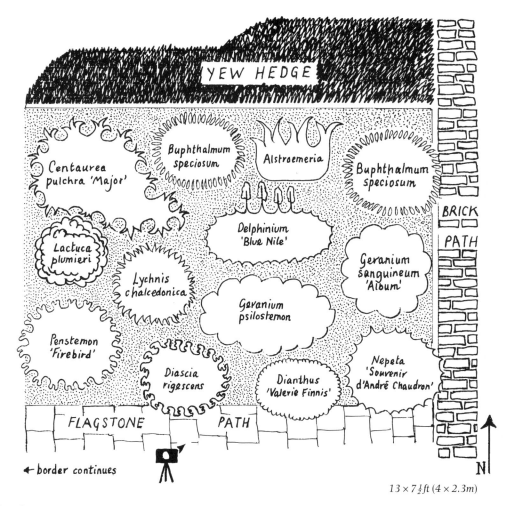

13 × 7½ ft (4 × 2.3m)

Plant list

Alstroemeria 'Ligtu Hybrids'
Buphthalmum speciosum
Centaurea pulchra 'Major'
Delphinium 'Blue Nile'
Dianthus 'Valerie Finnis'
Diascia rigescens

Geranium psilostemon, G. sanguineum 'Album'
Lactuca plumieri
Lychnis chalcedonica
Nepeta 'Souvenir d'André Chaudron'
Penstemon 'Firebird'

5 · Garden Conifers

A grass path disappears enticingly through a cluster of cypresses and junipers, inviting the gardener or visitor to enter a passage of blue and yellow greens and enjoy their resinous scents and hard, feathery foliage.

Hostas, lilies, ferns and alchemilla provide a herbaceous foreground in the same blue and yellow tones of green. Yellow poppies and primulas also draw attention to the yellow in the foliage of the golden cypress (*Chamaecyparis* 'Plumosa Aurea') and the thuja. The glaucous foliage of *Rosa rubrifolia* (*R.glauca*) blends perfectly with its nearest neighbours, accented in summer by its pale pink blooms.

Many people have decidedly strong feelings about conifers, either giving the entire garden over to them (apart from the spaces in between, which are saved for heathers), or else declaring their garden a conifer-free zone. Large gardens may be given a 'conifer corner', but it is more unusual to find a garden in which a serious attempt has been made to integrate them with herbaceous or shrubby companions. The results, as in the garden pictured here, can be dramatic without being showy.

Care should always be taken to find out the ultimate dimensions that conifers selected for the garden will reach. Some have a habit of growing very large, very fast and spoiling the carefully planned border – and possibly that of the neighbours as well.

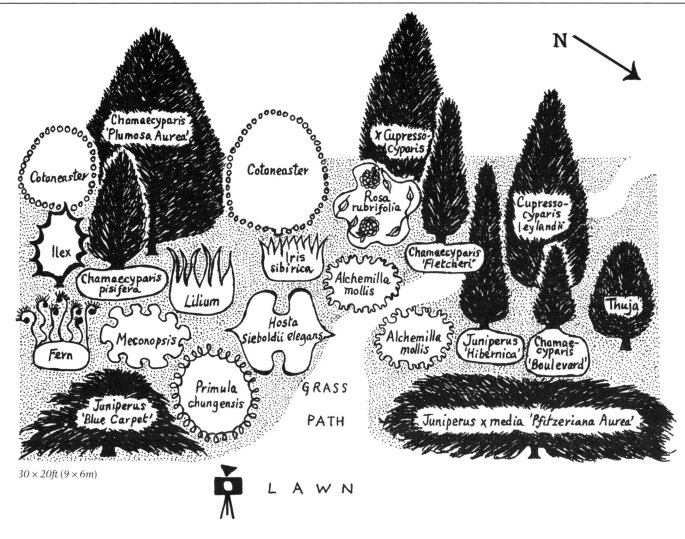

N

Chamaecyparis
'Plumosa Aurea'

Cotoneaster

Cotoneaster

× Cupresso-
cyparis

Ilex

Rosa
rubrifolia

Cupresso-
cyparis
leylandii

Chamaecyparis
pisifera

Iris
sibirica

Alchemilla
mollis

Chamaecyparis
'Fletcheri'

Lilium

Thuja

Fern

Meconopsis

Hosta
sieboldii elegans

Alchemilla
mollis

Juniperus
'Hibernica'

Chamae-
cyparis
'Boulevard'

Primula
chungensis

GRASS

PATH

Juniperus
'Blue Carpet'

Juniperus × media 'Pfitzeriana Aurea'

30 × 20ft (9 × 6m)

L A W N

Plant list

Alchemilla mollis
Chamaecyparis lawsoniana 'Fletcheri', C.pisifera
   'Boulevard' (2), C.'Plumosa Aurea'
Cotoneaster 'Cornubia' (2)
× Cupressocyparis leylandii
Dryopteris (fern)

Hosta sieboldii elegans
Ilex (holly)
Iris sibirica
Juniperus 'Blue Carpet', J.'Hibernica', J. × media
   'Pfitzeriana Aurea'
Lilium pardalinum

Meconopsis cambrica
Primula chungensis
Rosa rubrifolia (R.glauca)
Thuja occidentalis 'Rheingold'

6 · A Mixed Border

An acknowledged element of any mixed border is the contrast between the permanent and the temporary. Shrubs, whose image may change dramatically through the year, are permanent hosts to the transient appearances of their herbaceous neighbours.

In this border, a high yew hedge provides a constant evergreen backcloth for this shifting pattern of forms and colours. In spring, tulips, forget-me-nots and grape hyacinths are bright partners to the emerging foliage of white willows, golden elm and lilac. A little later on, apricot foxgloves mingle with the variegated foliage and pink flowers of the weigela, bold among the greens and greys of new summer growth.

Late in the summer, as pictured here, the orange-yellow daisy heads of anthemis rise above the pink flowers and dark foliage of *Hydrangea* 'Preziosa'. (Because the soil in this border is not very acid, the hydrangea produces flowers that are more red than purple.) Near by, the smoky-purple clouds of *Cotinus coggygria* 'Foliis Purpureis' help to structure the foreground. A formal link is provided by the giant umbels of *Allium christophii*; as these fade, the leaves are removed and the gap is filled with the annual *Cuphea* 'Firefly'.

There are many roses in this border; far from being kept in splendid isolation from other plants, as so often happens, they are allowed free association here with a wide diversity of admirable herbaceous and shrubby companions.

At the end of the year new introductions are planned and old acquaintances re-established or forsaken; the new season is never a repeat of the past.

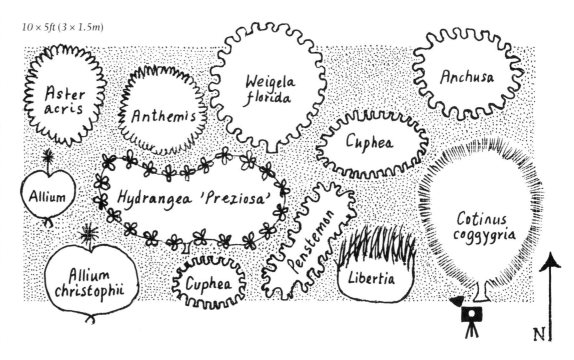

10 × 5ft (3 × 1.5m)

Plant list

Allium christophii
Anchusa azurea
Aster acris
Anthemis
Cotinus coggygria 'Foliis Purpureis'

Cuphea llavea miniata, C.l. 'Firefly'
Hydrangea 'Preziosa'
Libertia grandiflora
Penstemon 'Garnet'
Weigela florida 'Variegata'

Many of the best loved and deservedly famous old-fashioned roses are to be found in this garden. Bourbon, hybrid musk, gallica, centifolia, alba and moss roses dominate the four symmetrical beds; those that are compact and bushy are grown as free-standing shrubs, while others of laxer habit are trained up tripods or over hoops. All through the summer the air is scented with their short-lived pink, purple and magenta blooms. Their names recall the great French rose-breeders of the nineteenth century, their patrons and patrons' wives and mistresses, for, from Empire to Belle Epôque, France led the world in the cultivation of roses.

Gallica roses are undemanding in their soil requirements and tolerate some shade; 'Charles de Mills', 'Tuscany Superb' and 'Rosa Mundi' occupy beds III and IV, which are partly shaded by a birch. 'Belle de Crécy' and 'Cardinal Richelieu' thrive just as easily in the sunnier aspect of bed II. The Bourbons are represented by 'Honorine de Brabant' (whose creamy flowers are splashed with purple), 'Mme Isaac Pereire' and 'Mme Lauriol de Barny'.

The formality of the geometric design, with its neat box edging and the weeping pear standing at the crossing of the gravel paths, is complemented by a loosely symmetrical planting. This disposes seven or eight roses to each bed, together with two or three upward-trained clematis, two clumps of delphiniums and a variety of shrubs and herbaceous plants. Although at a first glance the planting appears to be dominated by the purple-blue-red colour range, on closer inspection the beds are more subtly colour-blocked. Bed II contains a sombre mixture of reds and purple-

blacks (*Iris chrysographes* and 'Liquorice Stick', *Viola* 'Molly Sanderson', and the damson-black *Helleborus orientalis*) which contrasts nicely with the paler blues and pinks of bed III.

(*Note*: The map is drawn facing west, whereas the photograph is taken facing south.)

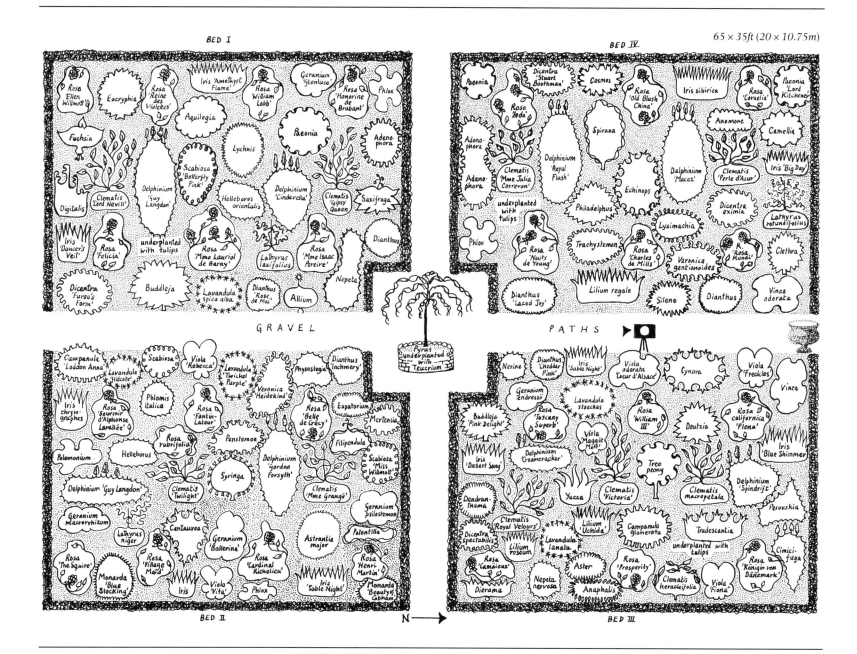

GRAVEL   PATHS

N →

BED II   BED III

Plant list

Adenophora forestii, *A.liliifolia*
Allium christophii
Anaphalis
Anemone
Aquilegia
Aster 'Violet Queen'
Astrantia major, *A.rubra*
Buddleja fallowiana, *B.*'Pink Delight'
Buxus sempervirens (hedges)
Camellia
Campanula glomerata, *C.lactiflora* 'Loddon Anna',
    C.takesimana
Centaurea 'John Coutts'
Cimicifuga ramosa
Clematis 'Gipsy Queen', *C.heracleifolia C.*'Lord
    Nevill', *C.macropetala*, *C.*'Madame Grangé',
    C.'Madame Julia Correvon', *C.*'Perle d'Azur',
    C.'Royal Velours', *C.*'Twilight', *C,*'Victoria'
Clethra alnifolia 'Paniculata'
Cosmos atrosanguineus
Cynara cardunculus
Delphinium 'Cinderella', *D.*'Creamcracker',
    D.'Gordon Forsyth', *D.*'Guy Langdon',
    D.'Macaz', *D.*'Royal Flush', *D.*'Spindrift'
Dendranthema 'Emperor of China'
Deutzia × elegantissima 'Rosealind'
Dianthus 'Cheddar Pink', *D.*'Inchmery', *D.*'Laced
    Joy', *D.*'Lilian', *D.*'Rose de Mai'
Dicentra eximia, *D.*'Furse's Form', *D.spectabilis*,
    D.'Stuart Boothman'
Dierama pulcherrimum
Digitalis × mertonensis
Echinops
Eucryphia × nymansensis
Eupatorium atropurpureum
Filipendula purpurea
Fuchsia
Geranium 'Ballerina', *G.endressii*, *G.*'Glenluce',
    G.macrorrhizum, *G.psilostemon*
Hebe 'Hagley Park'
Helleborus orientalis

Iris 'Amethyst Flame', *I.*'Big Day', *I.*'Blue
    Shimmer', *I.chrysographes*, *I.*'Dancer's Veil',
    I.'Desert Song', *I.* 'Liquorice Stick', *I.*'Sable
    Night', *I.sibirica*
Lathyrus laxifolius, *L.niger*, *L.rotundifolius*,
    L.sylvestris
Lavandula 'Hidcote', *L.lanata*, *L.spica alba*, *L.stoechas
    pedunculata*, *L.*'Twickel Purple'
Lilium regale, *L.speciosum album roseum*,
    L.speciosum album rubrum 'Uchida'
Lychnis coronaria
Lysimachia clethroides
Marrubium supinum
Mertensia virginica
Monarda 'Beauty of Cobham', *M.*'Blue Stocking'
Nepeta nervosa
Nerine
Paeonia 'Lord Kitchener', tree peony
Penstemon glaber
Perovskia atriplicifolia 'Blue Spire'
Philadelphus 'Belle Étoile'
Phlomis italica
Phlox (various)
Physostegia virginiana 'Alba'
Polemonium foliosissimum
Potentilla alba
Pyrus salicifolia 'Pendula'
Rosa 'Belle de Crécy', *R.californica* 'Plena',
    R.'Camäieux', *R.*'Cardinal Richelieu', *R.*'Charles
    de Mills', *R.*'Cornelia', *R.*'Ellen Willmott',
    R.'Fantin-Latour', *R.farreri persetosa*, *R.*'Felicia',
    R.'Henri Martin', *R.*'Honorine de Brabant',
    R.'Königin von Dänemark', *R.*'Leda',
    R.'Madame Isaac Pereire', *R.*'Madame Lauriol
    de Barny', *R.*'Rosa Mundi', *R.*'Nuits de Young',
    R.'Old Blush China', *R.*'Prosperity', *R.*'Reine des
    Violettes', *R.rubrifolia* (*glauca*), *R.*'Souvenir
    d'Alphonse Lavallée', *R.*'The Squire',
    R.'Tuscany Superb', *R.*'Village Maid',
    R.'William III', *R.*'William Lobb'
Saxifraga 'Miss Chamberlain'

Scabiosa 'Butterfly Blue', *S.*'Butterfly Pink', *S.*'Miss
    Willmott'
Silene maritima
Spiraea
Syringa
Teucrium
Trachystemon orientalis
Tradescantia
Veronica gentianoides, *V.*'Heidekind'
Vinca odorata
Viola 'Fiona', *V.*'Freckles', *V.*'Maggie Mott',
    V.'Molly Sanderson', *V.*'Coeur d'Alsace',
    V.'Rebecca', *V.*'Vita'
Yucca

Underplanted with tulips

8 · Town Garden

A pattern of silver, green and gold illuminates this border, so that even on the dullest days it seems to shine and beguiles the gardener while her hands are in the kitchen sink. Seen across a small cobbled courtyard, the raised border lies below a high grass bank in a steeply sloping town garden in Cornwall. The bank is retained by a 10ft (3m) concrete wall, painted cream and entirely smothered by ivies and clematis as well as a white wisteria, a vine, a rose, the golden hop and the hoary willow (*Salix elaeagnos*).

The ivies and the silvery green euonymus at the front of the border remain clothed throughout the year, so that even in deepest winter the pattern of green, silver and gold remains, accented by drifts of snowdrops. Lime-green hellebores, pale lemon narcissi and primroses usher in the spring, together with white brunneras and clematis. An underplanting of ranunculus and Welsh poppies (*Meconopsis cambrica*) and the new foliage of a potted acer carry the golden yellow theme into May. Summer sees the scented white racemes of the wisteria mingling with the creamy flowers of 'Madame Plantier', a sprawling shrub rose which, when trained to climb, can reach 12ft (4m). The golden filipendula brings colour into late summer and the euphorbia, Japanese anemones and white agapanthus take the border into autumn. Later in the season still, the primrose-yellow *Clematis rehderiana* and the cream-edged hostas ensure that colour lingers on into winter.

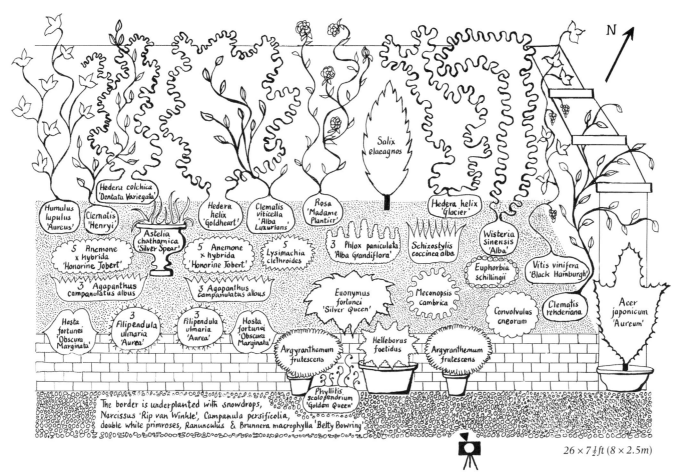

The labels within the illustration read:

Salix elaeagnos

Humulus lupulus 'Aureus'

Clematis 'Henryi'

Hedera colchica 'Dentata Variegata'

Astelia chathamica 'Silver Spear'

Hedera helix 'Goldheart'

Clematis viticella 'Alba Luxurians'

Rosa 'Madame Plantier'

Hedera helix 'Glacier'

Wisteria sinensis 'Alba'

5 Anemone × hybrida 'Honorine Jobert'

5 Anemone × hybrida 'Honorine Jobert'

5 Lysimachia clethroides

3 Phlox paniculata 'Alba Grandiflora'

Schizostylis coccinea alba

Euphorbia schillingii

Vitis vinifera 'Black Hamburgh'

3 Agapanthus campanulatus albus

3 Agapanthus campanulatus albus

Euonymus fortunei 'Silver Queen'

Meconopsis cambrica

Clematis rehderiana

Acer japonicum 'Aureum'

Convolvulus cneorum

Hosta fortunei 'Obscura Marginata'

3 Filipendula ulmaria 'Aurea'

3 Filipendula ulmaria 'Aurea'

Hosta fortunei 'Obscura Marginata'

Argyranthemum frutescens

Helleborus foetidus

Argyranthemum frutescens

Phyllitis scolopendrium 'Golden Queen'

The border is underplanted with snowdrops, Narcissus 'Rip van Winkle', Campanula persicifolia, double white primroses, Ranunculus & Brunnera macrophylla 'Betty Bowring'

N

26 × 7½ft (8 × 2.5m)

Plant list

Acer japonicum 'Aureum'
Agapanthus campanulatus albus (6)
Anemone × hybrida 'Honorine Jobert' (5 each side)
Argyranthemum frutescens (2)
Astelia chathamica 'Silver Spear'
Clematis 'Henryi', C.viticella 'Alba Luxurians',
    C.rehderiana
Convolvulus cneorum
Euonymus fortunei 'Silver Queen'
Euphorbia schillingii

Filipendula ulmaria 'Aurea' (6)
Hedera colchica 'Dentata Variegata', H.helix
    'Goldheart', H.helix 'Glacier'
Helleborus foetidus
Hosta fortunei 'Obscura Marginata'
Humulus lupulus 'Aureus'
Lysimachia clethroides (5 each side)
Meconopsis cambrica
Phlox paniculata 'Alba Grandiflora' (3)
Phyllitis scolopendrium 'Golden Queen'

Rosa 'Madame Plantier'
Salix elaeagnos
Schizostylis coccinea 'Alba'
Vitis vinifera 'Black Hamburgh'
Wisteria sinensis 'Alba'

Underplanted with Brunnera macrophylla 'Betty Bowring', Campanula persicifolia, snowdrops, Narcissus 'Rip Van Winkle', primroses (double white), ranunculus

An eighteenth-century Portland stone fountain in the shape of a monster fish occupies a niche in a wall clothed with ivies, cotoneaster and a vine. Water trickles gently over its rim into a shallow semi-circular pool, flanked on either side by large clumps of arum lilies. It is a sheltered, sunny corner of a terraced hillside garden swept by sea breezes; a favourite place for outdoor meals.

Red and white tulips open the flowering season, but the pattern of colours that follows is predominantly pastel. Apricot foxgloves are self-sown surprises and give height to the border. These are succeeded in late summer by the equally tall stems of *Verbena bonariensis*, whose tufty purple flowers linger on into autumn.

Many of the plants in this border are well known, and deservedly so, but a closer inspection reveals some unusual specimens. The low-growing *Marrubium cylleneum* 'Velvetissimum' (horehound) is a newcomer to the border; from July to September, soft purple flowers emerge from among its grey, felty leaves. Often described as 'undistinguished', it is overlooked by many gardeners. So, too, is *Malvastrum lateritium*, which has to live in poor soil if it is to give its best display of pale orange flowers. It must not be fed, otherwise it grows too big and gives but a poor show.

A few years ago an unfamiliar, mauve-flowered salvia was discovered growing in the garden; various experiments in propagation were made, from which it was found to come true from seed. Subsequently the salvia received its name from this garden: *Salvia patens* 'Chilcombe'.

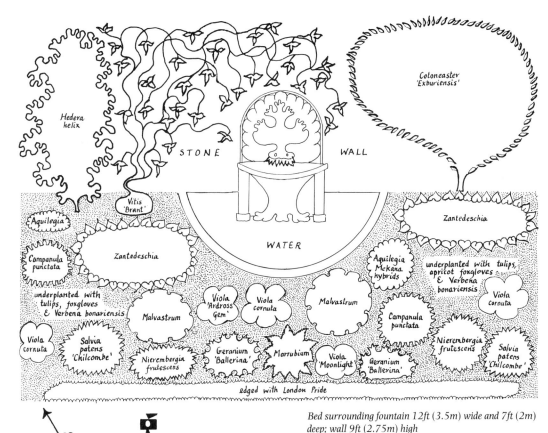

Bed surrounding fountain 12ft (3.5m) wide and 7ft (2m) deep; wall 9ft (2.75m) high

Plant list

Aquilegia 'McKana Hybrids' (2 clumps)
Campanula punctata (2)
Cotoneaster 'Exburiensis'
Geranium 'Ballerina' (2)
Hedera helix
Malvastrum lateritium (2)
Marrubium cylleneum 'Velvetissimum' (2)
Nierembergia frutescens (2)
Salvia patens 'Chilcombe' (several)
Saxifraga umbrosa (12) (London pride)

Viola 'Ardross Gem', *V.cornuta alba* (2),
  V. 'Moonlight' (2)
Vitis 'Brant'
Zantedeschia albomaculata (2)

Underplanted in April and May with water-lily tulips (red and white with dark green leaves), later with apricot foxgloves, and later still with *Verbena bonariensis*

This is one of four apple tunnels which together form a cross. It stands in a former rose garden, walled on three sides and with a river flowing by the fourth. At the centre of the cross, a number of ancient box balls surround a small pool. The tunnels are grand in scale, but the long narrow beds could well be shortened to suit a smaller garden.

The apple trees ('James Grieve', 'Lane's Prince Albert', 'Laxton's Superb', 'Newton Wonder' and 'Worcester Pearmain'), now twenty years old, have been espaliered to six tiers. This requires careful pruning in the summer, when all new growth is cut back to two buds from its origin, in order to form a fruiting spur. Although trees grown for this purpose are grafted on to a semi-dwarfing rootstock, growth here is so vigorous that the pruning often has to be repeated; the owner sometimes wishes that she had chosen less enthusiastic varieties.

The soil is chalky and apple trees are hungry plants; the beds need to be frequently fed and enriched with compost.

The semi-shaded beds beneath the apples are filled in springtime with pale yellow and white tulips (*Tulipa kaufmanniana* 'Shakespeare' and 'Heart's Delight' and *Tulipa* 'Spring Green') together with white polyanthus – colours that will not compete with the apple blossom. This is followed in the summer by a cool mixture of silver, green and grey foliage and muted shades of pink and purple flowers. Gaps are filled with bedding plants, such as nicotiana, ageratum, and diascia. In autumn a bright patch of colour is provided by Chinese lanterns (*Physalis alkekengi franchetii*).

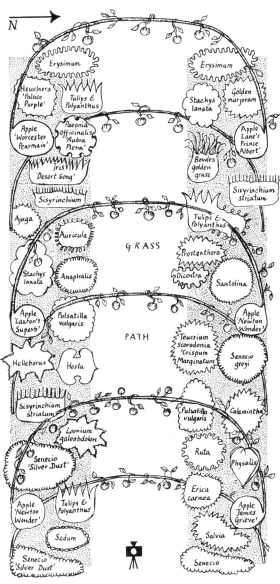

Plant list

Ajuga reptans 'Atropurpurea'
Anaphalis triplinervis (3)
Apple trees (6)
Auricula (7)
Calamintha nepeta
Dicentra spectabilis and *D.s.*'Alba' (3)
Erica carnea 'Springwood White'
Erysimum 'Bowles' Mauve' (3)
Helleborus corsicus, H.niger and *H.foetidus*
Heuchera 'Palace Purple' (3)
Hosta sieboldiana
Iris 'Desert Song' (7)
Lamium galeobdolon 'White Nancy'
Milium effusum aureum (Bowles' golden grass)
Oreganum vulgare aureum (golden marjoram)
Paeonia officinalis 'Rubra Plena' (3)
Physalis alkekengi franchetii (Chinese lantern)
Prostanthera lasianthos
Pulsatilla vulgaris (7)
Ruta graveolens (rue)
Salvia officinalis 'Variegata'
Santolina pinnata neapolitana
Sedum spurium
Senecio cineraria 'Silver Dust' and *S.greyi*
Sisyrinchium striatum
Stachys lanata (3)
Teucrium scorodonia 'Crispum Marginatum'

Underplanted with ageratum, dianthus, diascia, nicotiana, pansies, polyanthus and tulips.

Each bed 40ft × 3¾ft (12 × 1.15m); arches 9ft (2.75m) high

This is the tip of one of four curved beds divided by grass paths and backed by mature trees. In an otherwise brightly coloured mid-summer garden, this corner is an oasis of cool silvery greys and whites.

Many gardeners are attracted by the idea of making a white garden, but in practice it is not easy to achieve the desired effect for more than a short season. Large gardens may end up looking unfocused and washed out. Creating a small and secluded area where silver, white and cream can be shown off against a strong background of greens is a good solution.

Here the backcloth is provided by *Malus tschonoskii*, *Sorbus hupehensis* and *Cornus controversa*. Carefully chosen for their complementary foliage and habits, all three bear white flowers in early summer and, when the herbaceous plants in the foreground have faded, offer the distraction of flamboyant autumn colour.

In spring, a flock of white tulips among the newly emerging, glaucous leaves of *Hosta sieboldiana* announce the pattern of the season's colour. White foxgloves and the cloud of little white flowers of *Crambe cordifolia* follow, rising over white poppies, lupins and the silvery leaf rosettes of *Artemisia* × *latiloba* 'Valerie Finnis'. Later on in the summer, in a sunny and sheltered position, the shaggy white spikes of *Yucca filamentosa* contrast with the slender stems, grey leaves and white spires of *Lysimachia ephemerum*.

The soil here is clay, though not impossibly heavy, and quantities of mushroom compost have been incorporated. This improves the soil structure, but it also raises its pH, and it

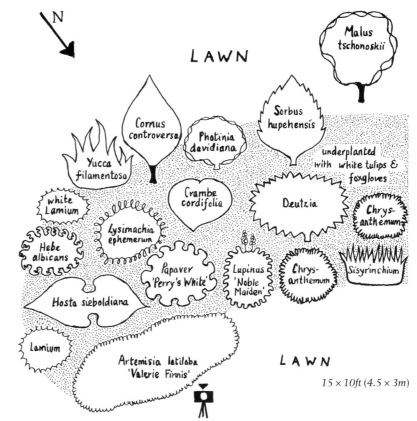

15 × 10ft (4.5 × 3m)

was feared that the foxgloves would not tolerate the alkaline environment. Foxgloves (which prefer shade and a soil that is on the acid side), however, are always prepared, it seems, to defy any soil and aspect.

Plant list

Artemisia × *latiloba* 'Valerie Finnis'
Chrysanthemum leucanthemum (ox-eye daisy) (2)
Cornus controversa
Crambe cordifolia
Deutzia scabra

Hebe albicans
Hosta sieboldiana
Lamium
Lupinus 'Noble Maiden'
Lysimachia ephemerum
Malus tschonoskii
Papaver orientale 'Perry's White'
Photinia davidiana 'Palette'
Sisyrinchium striatum
Sorbus hupehensis
Yucca filamentosa

Underplanted with white tulips and white foxgloves

12 · Towpath Garden

Lady Venice is a narrowboat moored in a central London canal basin. It belongs to a retired oil-rigger. He calls it 'a seaman's last moorings'.

The plants grow in cooking pans, buckets, wooden tubs, old chimney pots, a milk churn and numerous plastic containers which were originally designed to hold anything but plants. He makes drainage holes in their bases, fills them with 'any old earth' and occasionally feeds them. They are every-where: on the roof, on arches across the tow-path, hanging from railings and hooks. From March to early October the boat's royal blue paintwork is enveloped in colour.

He buys from market stalls, never from nurseries, but most of his plants are exchanged with friends in the neighbour-hood. In autumn he redoes it all and plants lots of bulbs. He overwinters some plants in a friend's greenhouse and buries his fuchsias horizontally under his towpath bed, where they clearly thrive. After the frosts he puts in his summer annuals and says he has no worries about colour subtlety. His favourites are dahlias, fuchsias, begonias and impatiens. *Lady Venice* is a tourist attraction that costs him £200 a year and two hours' work a week to maintain. At a time when plant theft is on the increase, these are fully protected by Bo'sun, his West Highland terrier.

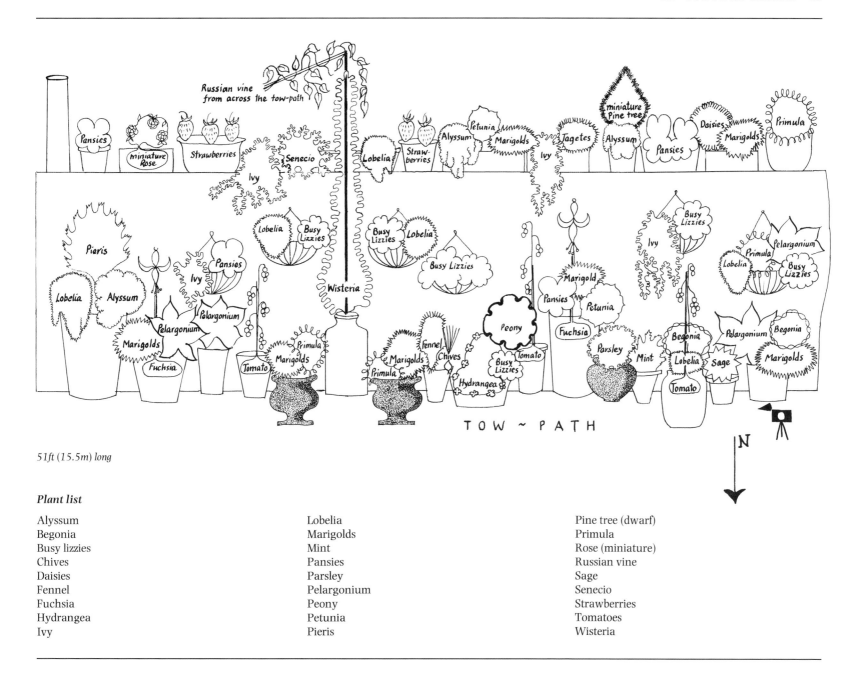

Russian vine from across the tow-path

Pansies

miniature Rose

Strawberries

Senecio

Ivy

Lobelia

Strawberries

Alyssum

Petunia

Marigolds

Ivy

Tagetes

Alyssum

Pansies

Daisies

Marigolds

Primula

miniature Pine tree

Pieris

Lobelia

Lobelia

Busy Lizzies

Busy Lizzies

Lobelia

Busy Lizzies

Ivy

Busy Lizzies

Ivy

Primula

Pelargonium

Lobelia

Alyssum

Ivy

Pansies

Lobelia

Busy Lizzies

Marigold

Pansies

Petunia

Pelargonium

Marigolds

Fuchsia

Pelargonium

Wisteria

Primula

Marigolds

Fennel

Chives

Peony

Fuchsia

Parsley

Mint

Begonia

Pelargonium

Begonia

Tomato

Marigolds

Primula

Busy Lizzies

Tomato

Lobelia

Sage

Marigolds

Hydrangea

Tomato

TOW ~ PATH

N

51ft (15.5m) long

Plant list

Alyssum	Lobelia	Pine tree (dwarf)
Begonia	Marigolds	Primula
Busy lizzies	Mint	Rose (miniature)
Chives	Pansies	Russian vine
Daisies	Parsley	Sage
Fennel	Pelargonium	Senecio
Fuchsia	Peony	Strawberries
Hydrangea	Petunia	Tomatoes
Ivy	Pieris	Wisteria

13 · A Small Conservatory

It is difficult to say whether it is best to enter a conservatory from the house or the garden; in each case the experience is quite different. Its success depends on a happy exploitation of the two approaches: entered from the controlled décor of the house it offers a riotous assembly of bold colours and forms that immediately engages the senses, while from the garden it presents a lush and exotic extension of an already familiar environment.

Viewed here from the house entrance, exuberant foliage and massed flowers create a luxuriant and perfumed enclosure which preludes the garden beyond. Vines and the more tender ivies make fine clothing for a conservatory wall. Growing a vine through other wall plants, however, can be tricky. Careful removal of selected shoots is essential if fruits are required, and during the summer months, when growth is wildly vigorous, checks must be made almost daily to ensure the viability of the vine's more discreet neighbours. Unless it is possible to put a special vine border inside (which permits the roots to travel outside), it is best to plant the vine outside the conservatory or glasshouse and then introduce it into the house via a hole near ground level.

The pelargonium is a deservedly popular summer plant. Grown in the ground in a sheltered situation such as this, it can reach heights of 2 metres or more, and grouped together in pots can provide a stunning show of colour from early summer through to late autumn. Frequent high potash feeds are essential.

At night, by lamplight, the green foliage and white blooms acquire a vibrancy that contrasts dramatically with their daytime appearance.

If space allows, citrus trees can transform the humblest lean-to conservatory into an 'orangery'. Given a large enough tub or pot they will grow to a height of 5 or 6 feet (up to 2 metres), but respond vigorously to hard pruning. Fragrant blossoms appear in spring, followed by fruits which ripen in winter. There is a drawback, however, for these lovely trees are amply provided with long and vicious thorns: moving them outside for the summer and bringing them back indoors for the winter can be a dismayingly heavy and dangerous task.

Plant list

Abutilon × *suntense*
Anisodontea capensis
Crassula
Fuchsia 'Royal Velvet', *F.* 'Swingtime' (2)
Hedera helix 'Anna Marie'
Nerine bowdenii 'Pink Triumph' (8)
Orange tree (dwarf)
Pelargonium 'Amour' (R), 'Aztec' (R), 'Billabong' (R), 'Carisbrooke' (R) (3), 'Chérie' (R) (3), 'Distinction' (Z), 'Dr A. Chipault' (ID) (cl), 'Fanny Eden' (R), 'Fascination' (R), 'Galilee' (ID) (cl), 'Grand Slam' (R), 'Lavender Grand Slam' (R) (2), 'Manx Maid' (A) (2), 'Rouletta' (I) (2) (cl), 'Senorita' (R), 'Tunias Perfecta' (R), 'White Chiffon' (R)
Plumbago auriculata
Vitis 'Black Hamburgh'

Pelargoniums: (R) Regal, (A) Angel, (Z) Zonal, (I) Ivy-leaved, (D) double, (cl) climbing

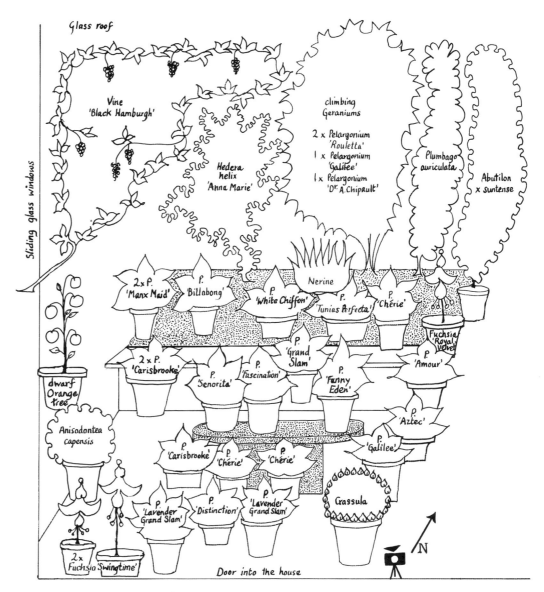

15 × 10ft (4.5 × 3m); height 10ft (3m)

This formal garden is enclosed by the walls of a medieval priory cloister. Its owners have enjoyed the considerable challenge of transforming it – as well as the house – into a contemporary work of art, without sacrificing the spiritual quality and serenity that have prevailed here for the last eight centuries.

As the map shows, there are really two gardens here, divided by a box hedge and linked by a central gateway, flanked with clipped hollies. Because the heights of the surrounding buildings differ, the two gardens, although loosely symmetrical, receive different quantities and qualities of light, and are planted accordingly. Structure and continuity are provided by eight Irish yews, which establish the formal rhythm of the garden.

Emphasis has been given to all-year colour and interest; an evergreen architecture of thuya, box, yew and *Lonicera nitida* frames a constantly changing pattern of forms and colours. In the coldest months, fragrant sarcococca and the winter cherry (*Prunus subhirtella* 'Autumnalis') flower against the shelter of the walls, while snowdrops and white hellebores mix with the silvery-grey foliage of santolina, lavender and artemisia. With the arrival of spring, the four standard forsythias are bright yellow above white tulips and lime-green hellebores and euphorbias. Early summer sees the wisteria and roses in bloom, surrounded by white and chartreuse irises; these are succeeded by lilies, white Michaelmas daisies and Japanese anemones, and bedded-out white cosmos. Hydrangeas and late-flowering clematis bring shades of pink, red and cream in the autumn.

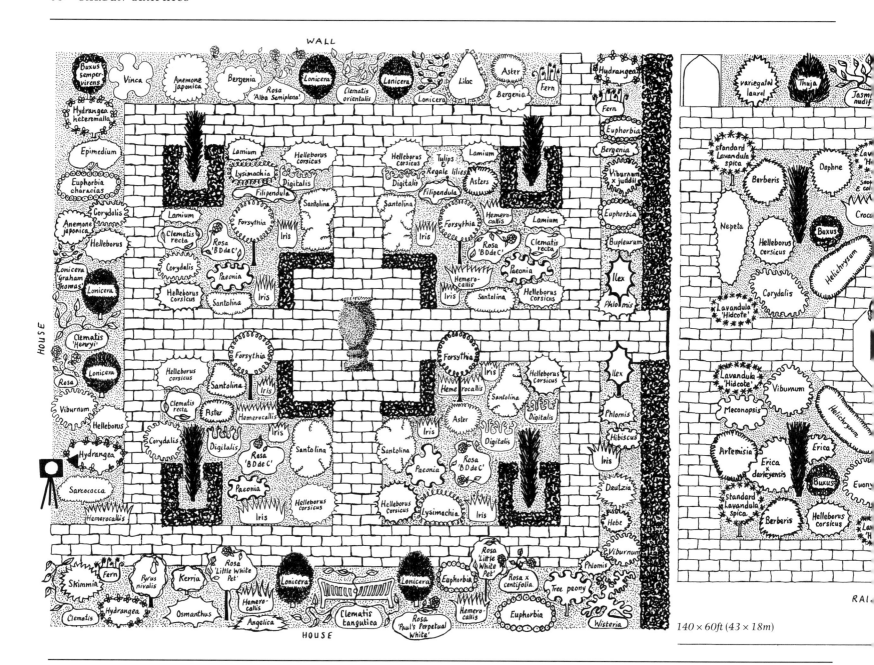

WALL

HOUSE

HOUSE

140 × 60ft (43 × 18m)

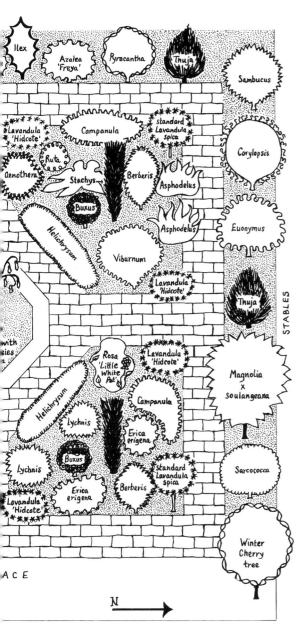

N →

STABLES

Plant list

Garden 1

SURROUNDING WALL BEDS

Anemone japonica (2)
Angelica archangelica (2)
Aster divaricatus
Bergenia 'Bressingham White' (3)
Bupleurum fruticosum
Buxus sempervirens (hedges)
Clematis montana 'Alexander', *C.tangutica*,
    C.'Henryi', *C.orientalis*
Corydalis wilsonii
Crocosmia 'Solfaterre' (2)
Deutzia setchuenensis
Epimedium perralderianum
Euphorbia palustris (2), *E.characias* (4)
Fern (4)
Hebe salicifolia
Helleborus orientalis
Hemerocallis flava (2)
Hibiscus 'Snowdrift'
Hydrangea 'Madame Emile Mouillère' (3),
    H.heteromalla
Ilex (holly) (2)
Iris 'Cleo' (8)
Kerria japonica 'Pleniflora'
Kniphofia 'Maid of Orleans'
Lonicera nitida 'Baggesen's Gold' (6), *L.*'Late
    Dutch', *L.*'Graham Thomas'
Melissa officinalis 'Aurea' (2)
Osmanthus × *burkwoodii*
Phlomis chrysophylla (2)
Pyrus nivalis
Rosa 'Alba Semiplena', *R.* × *centifolia*, *R.*'Little
    White Pet' (2), *R.*'Madame Legras de Saint
    Germain', *R.*'Paul's Perpetual White' (rambler)
Sarcococca
Skimmia laureola
Syringa (lilac)
Taxus baccata 'Fastigiata' (Irish yew) (4)
Tree peony
Viburnum farreri, *V.* × *juddii*, *V.tinus* 'Lucidum'

Vinca minor alba
Wisteria

INNER BEDS

Underplanted with snowdrops, tulips, *Anemone
blanda*, columbines, white foxgloves and *Lilium
regale*
Aster tradescantii
Clematis recta (4)
Corydalis wilsonii
Digitalis purpurea alba
Filipendula vulgaris
Forsythia (4)
Helleborus corsicus (4)
Hemerocallis citrina (4), *H.flava* (4)
Ilex aquifolium 'Bacciflava'
Iris 'Cleo' (8)
Lamium 'White Nancy'
Lysimachia nummularia 'Aurea' (4)
Paeonia 'Alba Plena' (4)
Rosa 'Blanc Double de Coubert' (4), *R.*'Little White
    Pet' (2)
Santolina (12)

Garden 2

SURROUNDING WALL BEDS

Corylopsis sinensis 'Spring Purple'
Euonymus fortunei 'Emerald Gaiety'
Helleborus niger 'Potter's Wheel'
Ilex aquifolium 'Clouded Gold'
Jasminum nudiflorum
Laurel (silver-variegated)
Magnolia soulangeana
Pyracantha
Rhododendron (*Azalea*) 'Freya'
Sambucus racemosa 'Plumosa Aurea'
Sarcococca 'Purple Stem'
Thuja occidentalis 'Rheingold' (3)
Winter cherry

INNER BEDS

Wisteria underplanted with campanula, crocuses
and pansies

contd

Artemisia canescens
Asphodelus luteus
Berberis 'Dart's Red Lady' (4)
Buxus sempervirens (4)
Campanula persicifolia
Corydalis cheilanthifolia
Crocosmia 'Solfaterre'
Daphne mezereum alba
Erica × *darleyensis* 'Molten Silver', *E.erigena* 'W.T. Rackliff'
Euonymus 'Emerald 'n' Gold'
Helichrysum angustifolium (2)
Helleborus corsicus
Lavandula 'Hidcote' (8), *L.spica* (4 standards)
Lychnis coronaria alba (2)
Meconopsis cambrica
Nepeta 'Six Hills Giant'
Oenothera
Rosa 'Little White Pet'
Ruta graveolens 'Jackman's Blue'
Stachys 'Cotton Boll'
Taxus baccata 'Fastigiata' (Irish yew) (4)
Viburnum farreri 'Nanum' (4)
Wisteria

Underplanted with snowdrops and columbines

Plant list

Abutilon 'Canary Bird'
Campanula isophylla
Clematis × *jackmannii*
Geranium 'Clorinda'
Helichrysum petiolatum
Lavandula spica (blue and pink lavender)
Papaver somniferum (opium poppy)
Rosa 'Iceberg'

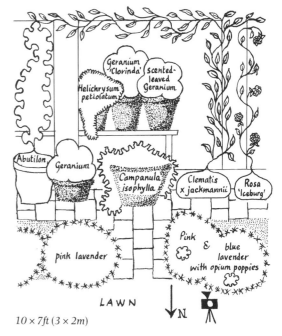

10 × 7ft (3 × 2m)

From July to October, *Clematis* × *jackmannii* produces an abundance of purple flowers on the current season's growth. Every year, in late winter or early spring, it is cut back to within 12 inches (25cm) of ground level; growth begins immediately and continues at astonishing speed. It shares a pillar with a climbing 'Iceberg' rose, whose brilliant white blooms contrast strikingly with the purple clematis. Both plants emerge from a mass of pink and blue lavender, which conceals bare or leggy lower stems.

Scented-leaved geraniums and trailing silver-grey helichrysum fill the pots beside the door and windows and stretch up to meet the clematis; stepping outside, the world seems purple and perfumed.

This old walled kitchen garden is divided into six square beds – one of which is shown on the plan – each filled with neat rows of vegetables. But this is more than a vegetable garden, for borders of flowering shrubs and perennials surround the beds. This combination has a practical as well as an aesthetic dimension: pollinating insects are encouraged and mono-cultural problems and diseases are deterred.

The mixed borders are planted by colour; this one covers the range of pinks, from pale-hued violas and geraniums, through the darker, though delicately shaded peony 'Sarah Bernhardt', to the rich purples of the sage and *Iris latifolia*. Contrasting splashes of creamy white come from the peony 'Duchesse de Nemours' and the philadelphus. Other borders contain viburnum and cornus, more sages, violas and geraniums, chosen to blend with the principal colour of the bed. Autumn colour is provided by sedums, Japanese anemones and the blue *Clematis heracleifolia*.

The garden is exposed to strong south-westerly winds, which means, in addition to a lot of watering, that the peonies need special treatment if they are not to be flattened by the first strong winds of the summer. As the new shoots emerge, lobster pots are placed over the crowns and anchored with pea sticks, which are soon hidden by the lush growth. These peonies were recently moved to their present position, in defiance of the belief that they hate root disturbance. A big hole and lots of manure often sweetens the sulkiest plants.

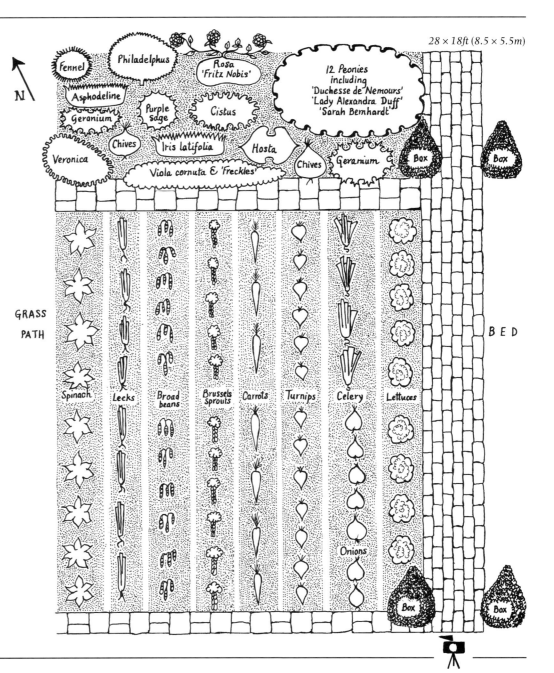

28 × 18ft (8.5 × 5.5m)

Plant list

The vegetable bed shown here has rows of spinach, leeks, broad beans, Brussels sprouts, carrots, turnips, celery, onions and lettuces

The flower bed at the top of the plan:
Asphodeline lutea
Box cones, clipped (4)
Chives (2 clumps)
Cistus
Fennel
Geranium × magnificum (2)
Hosta
Iris latifolia
Paeonia 'Duchesse de Nemours' (4), *P.* 'Lady
     Alexandra Duff' (4), *P.* 'Sarah Bernhardt' (4)
Philadelphus coronarius 'Variegatus'
Rosa 'Fritz Nobis'
Salvia (purple sage)
Veronica austriaca teucrium 'Crater Lake Blue'
Viola cornuta, V. 'Freckles'

Tarragon and golden marjoram (*Origanum vulgare aureum*) are planted in the flower bed to fill unexpected gaps

17 · A Cornish Pond

Successful waterside plantings, such as this one, depend on a planned variety of foliage, both in form and texture, because most marginal water plants flower in spring and early summer.

Stiff spikes of iris contrast with the softer verticals of the variegated oat grass (*Arrhenatherum*) and the rushes (*Juncus* and *Scirpus*), and with the flat lily pads, arum spathes and feathery astilbe. While other flowers fade and the arum spathes give way to bright orange fruits, the astilbe plumes keep their form even in winter. The blue spikes of the pickerel weed bring a new wave of colour in July and August.

If space were less confined, a planting of houttuynia would give a cloud of pink and white on delicate stems throughout the summer and into early autumn. Ornamental dogwoods with their bright stems would provide winter colour (*Cornus alba* and *Cornus stolonifera* 'Flaviramea'). Cotula, aptly known as 'brass buttons', tolerates its crown remaining below water level and would grow well on the inner shelf at the water's edge.

Although this garden pond is in a mild and sheltered area, all the plants are fully hardy with the exception of the tender shamrock pea (*Parochetus communis*), which is more often seen in the shelter of an alpine house.

The pond divides the house from the lawn. It measures 25ft × 13ft (7.5m × 4m) with a water depth of 2ft 6in (75cm). The top of the low surrounding wall is made of flagstones and is a good height for sitting on. Curved corners soften the rectangle.

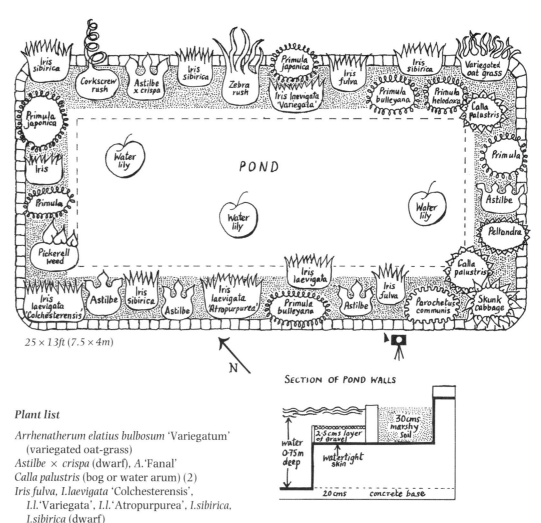

25 × 13ft (7.5 × 4m)

N

SECTION OF POND WALLS

Plant list

Arrhenatherum elatius bulbosum 'Variegatum'
  (variegated oat-grass)
Astilbe × crispa (dwarf), *A.* 'Fanal'
Calla palustris (bog or water arum) (2)
Iris fulva, I.laevigata 'Colchesterensis',
  I.l. 'Variegata', *I.l.* 'Atropurpurea', *I.sibirica,*
  I.sibirica (dwarf)
Juncus effusus 'Spiralis' (corkscrew rush)
Lysichiton americanus (skunk cabbage)
Nymphaea alba, N.tuberosa 'Richardsonii'
Parochetus communis
Peltandra undulata
Pontederia cordata (pickerel weed)

Primula bulleyana, P.helodoxa, P.japonica
Scirpus lacustris tabernaemontani 'Zebrinus' (zebra
  rush)

6–10 irises and primulas are recommended for each clump

Where flowerbeds meet grass, plants have to be kept back from the edge, or else mowing becomes tedious; but wherever they are bordered by a path it is a relief and a pleasure to allow them to spill over the frontier and soften the contours of brick, stone or gravel.

This border, which receives the benefit of full sun and good drainage, is a perfect home to rosemary, lavender, *Convolvulus cneorum* and the poached-egg flower (*Limnanthes douglasii*), all of which are allowed to fall over the flint and flagstone path. This is nicely balanced by the more contained and upright forms of the irises, chives and penstemons.

Narrow borders can be problematic, and it is always worth considering whether their width is justified by an existing structure or proportions, or is merely the whim of an unimaginative or lazy gardener. In some cases it may be better to do away with the border altogether than submit to the mean constraints of an unsuitable location.

At the foot of a wall, for example, a kind of Vitruvian principle might be applied which widens the border proportionately to the height of the wall. (An exception to this would be the sort of very narrow border employed only for growing climbers or wall-trained shrubs and trees.) Borders unsupported by a wall or hedge which flank or are flanked by paths need to follow a similar principle: a grand avenue flanked by skimpy borders is clearly inappropriate.

Once the width of the border has been determined, suitable planting, in terms of height and bulk, is essential. While wide borders can be stacked at the back with delphiniums and verbascums, narrow borders

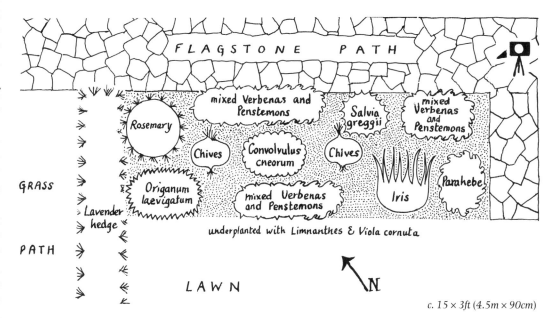

c. 15 × 3ft (4.5m × 90cm)

demand greater restraint and lower, less exuberant plants. Vertical accents should not be ignored, however, provided they match the scale of the surrounding planting.

Plant list

Centaurea
Chives (4)
Convolvulus cneorum (2)
Iris
Lamium 'Variegatum'
Lavandula 'Munstead' (hedge)
Origanum laevigatum (2)
Parahebe catarractae (2)
Penstemon 'Purple Bedder', *P.* 'Garnet'
Potentilla × *hopwoodiana*
Rosa 'Baron Girod de l'Ain'
Rosemary
Salvia greggii (2)
Verbena 'Silver Anne', *V.* 'Sissinghurst'

Underplanted with *Limnanthes douglasii* (poached egg plant) and *Viola cornuta*

A whitewashed wall capped with red pantiles, terracotta and painted pots overflowing with bright colours and lush foliage, scented evening air – the feeling is unmistakably Mediterranean.

Some carefully chosen shrubs and climbers occupy the largest containers in the background. *Rosa chinensis* 'Mutabilis' is an unusual rose of medium height and graceful habit; its crimson flowers are highly scented. Beside it, the aromatic, silvery-grey leaves of *Artemisia absinthium* intertwine with the softer, feltier grey of helichrysum. Clematis and honeysuckle need canes and wires to help them scramble up the wall; clematis also looks lovely if allowed to trail over the edge of its container (provided molluscs can be kept at bay).

Perhaps the headiest scent comes from the pot of lilies in the foreground; on a still evening their scent can be overwhelming.

It is important, when plants are growing in artificial, containerized conditions, to give them all the assistance they need in order to perform well. Good compost that drains well is the first requirement. Loam-based composts retain moisture longer and dry out less catastrophically than peat-based mixtures, but they are much heavier, a factor that should be taken into consideration if the pots have to be moved. Watering has to be built into a daily routine that can become a tedious chore if a tap is not close to hand or if hosepipe bans are being enforced. Feeding at weekly or twice-weekly intervals during the flowering season is also important: potassium (potash) will encourage lush blooms over a longer period. The woody plants which remain in their pots

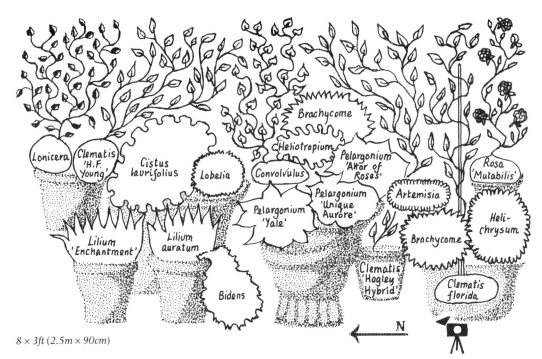

8 × 3ft (2.5m × 90cm)

all year (the honeysuckle, clematis, cistus and rose) need extra feeding to see them through the winter months. At the start of spring, it is a good idea to remove the top few inches of compost, sprinkle with powdered blood, fish and bone, and then top the pots up with fresh compost.

Plant list

Artemisia 'Lambrook Silver'
Bidens ferulifolia
Brachycome multifida (2)
Cistus laurifolius
Clematis florida 'Flore Pleno', *C.* 'Hagley Hybrid', *C.* 'H.F. Young'
Helichrysum petiolare
Heliotropium 'Princess Marina'
Ipomoea tricolor
Lilium auratum, L. 'Enchantment'
Lobelia erinus 'Sapphire'
Lonicera periclymenum 'Serotina'
Pelargonium 'Attar of Roses', *P.* 'Unique Aurore', *P.* 'Yale'
Rosa × *odorata* 'Mutabilis'

20 · Mill Pool Bank

Built on a terraced slope, this is both a rockery and a poolside garden. Consequently the soil is as free-draining as it is moist, and offers the possibility of a more varied planting scheme than that allowed by a more moisture-retentive soil. So, in addition to the rheums and rodgersias, the primulas and pelti-phyllums – all poolside *habitués* – there are senecios and buphthalmum, geraniums and euphorbias, as well as two tall, conical junipers which all prefer a well-drained, even dryish soil.

A flagstone path, which threads along the water's edge, interrupted by the two streams which chase down the slope over the shallow stone terraces, affords a closer view of the planting scheme. Beneath the junipers, mottled green tolmiea hugs the ground, sharing the cool shade with the creamy yellow flowers of the foxglove (*Digitalis ambigua*); a cascade of yellow mimulus cuts across the path, and, looking across the water to the low wall which separates the pool from the yard, perennials and ferns, chosen for their leaf texture, reach down to the water's edge.

In June, when the bank is at its most spectacular, reds, pinks and yellows predominate, harmonized by the background foliage of greens, blues and greys.

The white water lilies are at a disadvantage in the turbulent water of a mill race pool, and would flower much better in still water.

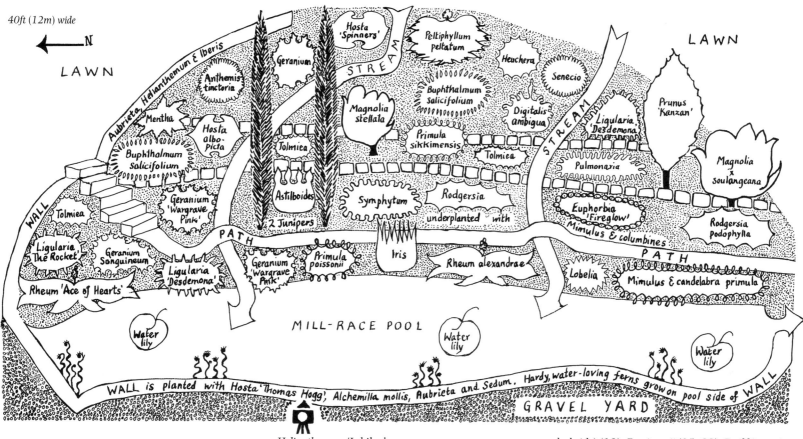

40ft (12m) wide

N

LAWN

LAWN

Aubrieta, Helianthemum & Iberis

Anthemis tinctoria

Mentha

Hosta albo-picta

Buphthalmum salicifolium

Geranium

Hosta 'Spinners'

Peltiphyllum peltatum

Heuchera

Senecio

STREAM

Buphthalmum salicifolium

Digitalis ambigua

STREAM

Prunus 'Kanzan'

Magnolia stellata

Primula sikkimensis

Tolmiea

Ligularia 'Desdemona'

Magnolia x soulangeana

Tolmiea

Geranium 'Wargrave Pink'

Astilboides

2 Junipers

Tolmiea

Symphytum

Rodgersia underplanted with

Pulmonaria

Euphorbia 'Fireglow'

Rodgersia podophylla

WALL

PATH

Ligularia 'The Rocket'

Geranium sanguineum

Ligularia 'Desdemona'

Geranium 'Wargrave Pink'

Primula poissonii

Iris

Rheum alexandrae

Mimulus & columbines

PATH

Lobelia

Mimulus & candelabra primula

Rheum 'Ace of Hearts'

Water lily

MILL-RACE POOL

Water lily

Water lily

WALL is planted with Hosta 'Thomas Hogg', Alchemilla mollis, Aubrieta and Sedum. Hardy, water-loving ferns grow on pool side of WALL

GRAVEL YARD

Plant list

Alchemilla mollis

Anthemis tinctoria 'E.C. Buxton', *A.t.* 'Grallach Gold', *A.t.* 'Kelwayi'

Astilboides tabularis

Aubrieta

Buphthalmum salicifolium

Digitalis ambigua

Euphorbia 'Fireglow'

Ferns

Geranium endressii 'Wargrave Pink', *G.sanguineum lancastrense*

Helianthemum 'Jubilee'

Heuchera

Hosta 'Albopicta', *H.*'Spinners', *H.*'Thomas Hogg'

Iberis sempervirens

Iris pseudacorus 'Variegata'

Juniperus communis 'Hibernica' (2)

Ligularia dentata 'Desdemona', *L.przewalskii* 'The Rocket'

Lobelia vedrariensis

Magnolia × soulangeana, *M.stellata*

Mentha × gentilis 'Variegata'

Peltiphyllum peltatum (8–10)

Primula beesiana and *P.pulverulenta* (candelabra

hybrids) (12), *P.poissonii* (15–20), *P.sikkimensis* (15–20)

Prunus 'Kanzan'

Pulmonaria saccharata alba (8)

Rheum 'Ace of Hearts', *R.alexandrae*

Rodgersia podophylla

Sedum

Senecio

Symphytum × uplandicum 'Variegatum'

Tolmiea menziesii 'Taff's Gold'

Water lilies (hardy, white)

Underplanted with columbines, mimulus and *Hypericum elatum*

A four-square yew hedge encloses this historic garden at Hatfield House, Hertfordshire, and separates it from the parkland and larger garden which lie outside. It serves to remind us that gardens are defined by their boundaries in more than one sense – the word 'garden', like the French '*jardin*', derives, with terms such as 'girth' and 'yard', from the Sanskrit '*gerdh*', meaning an encircling boundary.

Too large and formal to feel like a truly 'secret garden', this is, nevertheless, a secluded and peaceful place; a geometric pattern of beds, connected and softened by grass paths, radiates from a round pool and fountain, so that the sound of splashing water is never far away.

The beds are filled with roses, peonies, irises and a wide variety of herbaceous plants, supported, where necessary, by a twiggy framework; the overall effect is a billowing profusion of purples, pinks, blues and yellows. Deep blue *Veronica teucrium* combines stunningly with the pale pink, double blooms of *Paeonia* 'Marie Crousse' and a little later with the purple-red shrub rose 'Cardinal Hume'. A low skirt of the uncommon *Geranium sessiflorum nigricans* creates a sprinkling of white flowers at ground level, and balances the white sprays of gypsophila that float in the background.

Many of the cultivars here are rare or unusual, and make this a plantsman's garden. The penstemon 'Sour Grapes' is the subject of an amusing note by Beth Chatto in her catalogue of unusual plants. She writes: 'I feel sentimental about this plant which was given me, under this name, by Vita Sackville-West. I am told that it should be called 'Stapleford

Gem'. Having sent out possibly thousands as 'Sour Grapes' I am reluctant to change and confuse many gardeners. [It] is a beautiful plant, hardy on well-drained soil. The flowers are like unripe grapes or opals, soft green, amethyst and blue, opening from July till October.'

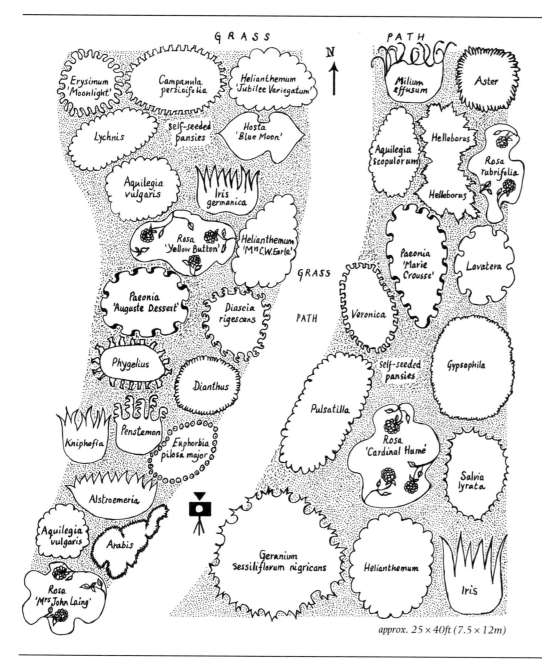

GRASS

PATH

N

Erysimum 'Moonlight'

Campanula persicifolia

Helianthemum 'Jubilee Variegatum'

Milium effusum

Aster

Lychnis

self-seeded pansies

Hosta 'Blue Moon'

Aquilegia scopulorum

Helleborus

Rosa rubrifolia

Aquilegia vulgaris

Iris germanica

Helleborus

Rosa 'Yellow Button'

Helianthemum 'Mrs C.W. Earle'

Paeonia 'Marie Crousse'

Lavatera

GRASS

Paeonia 'Auguste Dessert'

Diascia rigescens

PATH

Veronica

Phygelius

Dianthus

self-seeded pansies

Gypsophila

Penstemon

Pulsatilla

Kniphofia

Euphorbia pilosa major

Rosa 'Cardinal Hume'

Salvia lyrata

Alstroemeria

Aquilegia vulgaris

Arabis

Geranium sessiliflorum nigricans

Helianthemum

Iris

Rosa 'Mrs John Laing'

approx. 25 × 40ft (7.5 × 12m)

Plant list

Alstroemeria psittacina pulchella
Aquilegia vulgaris, A.scopulorum
Arabis 'Old Gold'
Aster novi-belgii
Campanula persicifolia 'Telham Beauty'
Dianthus 'Village Pink'
Diascia rigescens
Erysimum 'Moonlight'
Euphorbia × martinii, E.pilosa major
Geranium sessiliflorum nigricans
Gypsophila 'Rosy Veil'
Helianthemum 'Highdown', H.'Jubilee
 Variegatum', H.'Mrs C.W. Earle'
Helleborus 'Boughton Beauty'
Hosta 'Blue Moon'
Iris germanica, I.'Soft Blue'
Kniphofia 'Percy's Pride'
Lavatera arborea
Lychnis × haageana
Milium effusum 'Aureum'
Paeonia 'Auguste Dessert', P.'Marie Crousse'
Penstemon 'Sour Grapes'
Phygelius aequalis albus
Pulsatilla vulgaris
Rosa 'Cardinal Hume', R.'Mrs John Laing',
 R.rubrifolia (R.glauca), R.'Yellow Button'
Salvia lyrata
Veronica teucrium

Self-sown pansies

A low hedge of clipped box frames this bed, but this external formality is contrasted with an internal informality in which shades of green and cream play over a variety of textures and forms throughout the summer.

The planting is dominated by two large clumps of gypsophila which, in soil that is alkaline and well-drained, produces a cloud of tiny white flowers, borne above grassy leaves on thin stems. Ornamental cabbages, raised as hardy annuals, are eye-catching without being gaudy. The green and cream annual *Euphorbia marginata* would look equally well here.

In recent years, the complementary interest in garden restoration and enthusiasm for formal gardens have led to a quiet revival of the box-edged parterre. The small leaves and dense habit of dwarf box make it amenable to very precise clipping, enabling patterns to be drawn with firm, distinct and uniform definitions. In the seventeenth century, geometric designs of stunning complexity, best viewed from an upstairs window, exploited the neat conformity of box to the full. There was little emphasis on other plants: geometric compartments were kept empty, or filled with coloured gravels, to emphasize the intricacy of the pattern. This bears little relation to the present-day parterre, which favours simple geometric shapes, packed with flowers, vegetables or herbs.

Plant list

Brassica oleracea
Gypsophila paniculata (3)
Nicotiana affinis
Petunia (*multiflora* and *grandiflora*) *Polygonum*
Verbascum

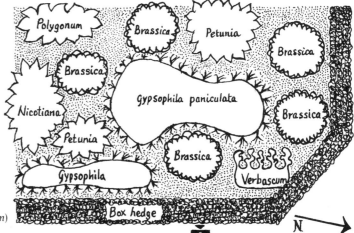

10 × 6ft (3 × 1.8m)

This awkward bed – only 4ft square and shaded – provides clear evidence that no part of the garden, however unpromising, need be ignored. Obviously it would be unwise to imagine that it could provide all-year-round colour and interest, but by focusing on one extended season (May to August) and a simplified range of forms and colours, a luxuriant and arresting effect has been achieved.

The slow-growing, glaucous *Hosta tokudama* sets the tone; its broad, cup-shaped leaves create an unfussy block of colour, modulated by light and shade. Similarly, *Alchemilla mollis* is visually uncomplicated; discreet greenish-yellow flowers are borne on slender stems above the pale green leaves. Its leaves are hairy and delicately toothed and sparkle with dew in the morning. *Tellima grandiflora* is just as simple and arresting: a clump of heart-shaped leaves which in late spring is overhung with tiny white flowers – like a spray of water.

However, simple monochrome blocks of green need to be accented if their arresting simplicity is to be appreciated. In spring, purple, pink and white columbines emerge among the foliage; later on in the summer, dwarf irises provide foreground detail while the herbaceous *Clematis integrifolia* produces a background of bright blue flowers. The turks-cap blooms of the tiger lilies, orange spotted with purple, bring the season to a dramatic close.

All the plants in this bed thrive in shade or semi-shade, but will do poorly in soil that is not well drained. A small area that is perpetually moist as well as shaded presents different opportunities: a collection of ferns,

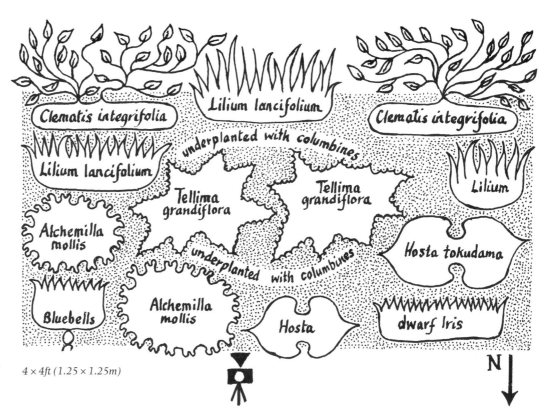

4 × 4ft (1.25 × 1.25m)

for example, might prove a happy addition that could transform the attitude of the gardener towards the dankest corner of his or her garden.

Gardening in the shade has its own rewards, as everyone who has stepped into a garden at dusk will know: pale colours gleam and foliage acquires a deeper, darker shade of green. The cooler temperature induces an atmosphere of tranquillity, making the hectic colours of the bright and sunlit garden seem far away.

Plant list

Alchemilla mollis
Bluebells
Clematis integrifolia
Hosta tokudama
Iris (dwarf)
Lilium lancifolium (tiger lilies)
Tellima grandiflora

Underplanted with self-sown columbines

The designer of this garden has drawn upon both French and English kitchen garden styles. The geometrical pattern of parterres which structures the design is inspired by French formality, and in particular by the ornamental *jardin potager* at Villandry, in the Loire valley. Very English, on the other hand, are the colourful and informal plant associations, which would have had no place at Villandry.

Each of the sixteen beds is edged with lavender. (Villandry's beds are austerely edged with clipped box.) Here, the inner four are edged with pink *Lavandula angustifolia* 'Rosea' and the outer twelve with purple *L.*'Munstead'. Inside, the beds are filled with vegetables grown as much for their bold foliage as for their culinary uses (such as artichokes, ruby chard, and purple cabbage), with small evergreen shrubs, bright flowering perennials and, in summer, bright patches of annuals. The marigolds and nasturtiums have a practical function too – marigolds are reputed to keep whitefly at bay, while nasturtiums focus the attention of blackfly. The owners have also been growing oriental vegetables, as they have a keen interest in Thai cooking, but although these have become more available lately, many do not like this garden's cold, wet loam.

The idea of mixed planting is continued up, along and under the walls. Climbing roses and other flowering shrubs are interspersed with fruit trees and bushes.

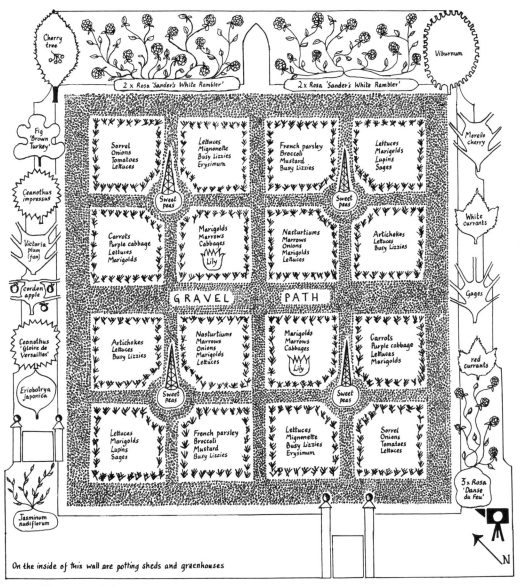

Cherry tree

Viburnum

2 x Rosa 'Sander's White Rambler'

2 x Rosa 'Sander's White Rambler'

Fig 'Brown Turkey'

Morello cherry

Sorrel
Onions
Tomatoes
Lettuces

Lettuces
Mignonette
Busy Lizzies
Erysimum

French parsley
Broccoli
Mustard
Busy Lizzies

Lettuces
Marigolds
Lupins
Sages

Ceanothus impressus

White currants

Sweet peas

Sweet peas

Carrots
Purple cabbage
Lettuces
Marigolds

Marigolds
Marrows
Cabbages
Lily

Nasturtiums
Marrows
Onions
Marigolds
Lettuces

Artichokes
Lettuces
Busy Lizzies

Victoria plum (fan)

Cordon apple

GRAVEL   PATH

Gages

Artichokes
Lettuces
Busy Lizzies

Nasturtiums
Marrows
Onions
Marigolds
Lettuces

Marigolds
Marrows
Cabbages
Lily

Carrots
Purple cabbage
Lettuces
Marigolds

Ceanothus 'Gloire de Versailles'

red currants

Sweet peas

Sweet peas

Eriobotrya japonica

Lettuces
Marigolds
Lupins
Sages

French parsley
Broccoli
Mustard
Busy Lizzies

Lettuces
Mignonette
Busy Lizzies
Erysimum

Sorrel
Onions
Tomatoes
Lettuces

3 x Rosa 'Danse du Feu'

Jasminum nudiflorum

On the inside of this wall are potting sheds and greenhouses

N

68 × 68ft (20.5 × 20.5m)

Plant list

VEGETABLE BEDS
The hedges of the twelve outer beds:
Lavandula 'Munstead'
The hedges of the four inner beds:
Lavandula angustifolia 'Rosea'
In the beds are artichokes, broccoli, busy lizzies,
purple cabbages, carrots and *Erysimum* 'Bowles'
Mauve', French parsley, lettuces, lilies, lupins,
marigolds, marrows, mignonette, mustard,
nasturtiums, onions, sages, sorrel, sweet peas
and tomatoes

WALL SHRUBS AND FRUIT TREES/BUSHES
Apple trees – fanned and cordonned
Ceanothus 'Gloire de Versailles', *C.impressus*
Eriobotrya japonica
Fig 'Brown Turkey'
Gages
Jasminum nudiflorum
Morello cherry tree (2)
Redcurrants (10)
Rosa 'Danse du Feu', *R.* 'Sander's White
    Rambler' (4)
Viburnum rhytidophyllum
Victoria plum (fan)
White currants (10)

BEDS BELOW THE WALLS
Alstroemeria ligtu, Catananche caerulea (Cupid's
dart), cornflowers, *Erigeron* 'Pink Jewel', *Helleborus
orientalis*, gladiolus (white), gooseberries,
gypsophila, nasturtiums, peonies, phlox, poppies,
rhubarb, scabious, wild strawberries and veronica

This is one of several small beds in a sheltered courtyard garden in the Midlands. The gardener, who is both a photographer and a plantsman, has composed a miniature in shades of purple, blue, green and grey which spills over the frame of stone slabs and gravel.

Phuopsis stylosa deserves to be better known: it thrives in dry, sunny situations and, in early summer, produces masses of rich pink 'pincushions', as Beth Chatto so aptly describes them. Here it flourishes among silver thyme and lavender, which show off its amethyst flowers to great effect. Taller spires of flax, camassia and irises lend height and depth to the composition. In spring, a carpet of jewel-like scillas, crocuses, narcissi and muscari surround the dwarf junipers.

Underplanting with bulbs is a very effective way of extending the flowering season of small beds such as this, where spring- or autumn-flowering perennials or shrubs would overcrowd the limited space and spoil the simplicity of the design. It is best to put the bulbs in after the bed has been planted up so that they are not disturbed or damaged. Lifting and dividing perennials in later years will lead to some disturbance, but this simply cannot be avoided.

Autumn-flowering bulbs make a welcome addition to any border: colchicums and zephyranthes require only a small space at the front of the border, where they will shine with a spring-like intensity among the faded blooms of summer and richer tints of autumn.

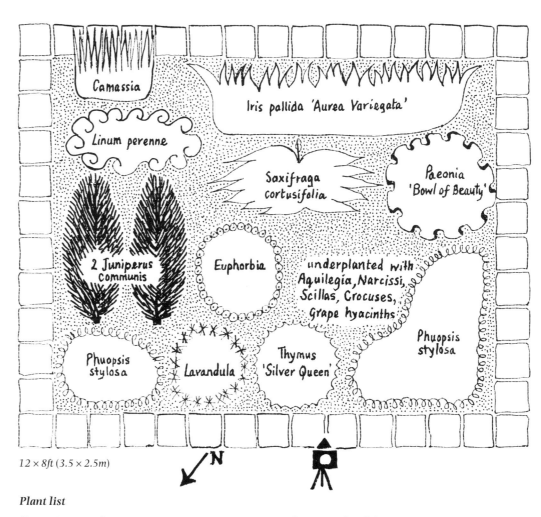

12 × 8ft (3.5 × 2.5m)

Plant list

Camassia quamash
Euphorbia amygdaloides 'Variegata'
Iris pallida 'Aurea Variegata'
Juniperus communis 'Compressa' (2)
Lavandula
Linum perenne
Paeonia lactiflora 'Bowl of Beauty'

Phuopsis stylosa (2)
Saxifraga cortusifolia fortunei 'Rubrifolia'
Thymus 'Silver Queen'

Underplanted with columbines, crocuses, grape hyacinths, narcissi and scillas

Front gardens have a character and an appeal of their own. In towns, whether used as a repository for dustbins and bicycles or designed as a gloriously planted frontispiece, the front garden is a buffer zone between street and front door. In the country, however, the front garden takes on a different aspect, altogether more open and inviting. In contrast to the city garden, the country front garden includes the passer-by. Such is the case here: between the white picket fence and the clapboard house a cottage-style profusion of colour provides a charming introduction which welcomes visitors and passers-by alike.

The soil is less welcoming: it is poor and stony, and only tough plants will survive here. Old-fashioned, heavily scented pinks thrive; *Dianthus* 'Mrs Sinkins', with double white and endearingly fringed blooms, is a favourite. Single-flowered pinks seed themselves with abandon, and violas also pop up everywhere. *Viola cornuta*, planted near the intriguing *V.*'Bowles' Black', together with a selection of purple, white and yellow violas, results in an interesting batch of self-sown seedlings each year.

An American native, *Eriophyllum lanatum* never fails to impress with its bright yellow daisy flowers that suddenly overwhelm its subdued grey foliage. It has to be kept well away from the magenta *Lychnis viscaria*, which glories in the common name of 'sticky Nellie'.

Prunella webbiana (self-heal) spreads and seeds rather too enthusiastically; it has purple flowers, while *P.w.*'Pink Loveliness' is pale lilac. But together they are so pretty that territorial ambitions are forgiven.

Plant list

Ajuga reptans
Alyssum saxatile 'Dudley Neville'
Anthemis cupaniana
Arabis caucasica
Armeria alliacea 'Formosa Hybrids'
Cerastium tomentosum (snow-in-summer)
Consolida ajacis (larkspur)
Convolvulus sabatius
Cotoneaster horizontalis
Crepis incana
Dianthus 'Dad's Favourite', *D.*'Mrs Sinkins'
Erigeron 'Dimity'
Eriophyllum lanatum
Erysimum 'Bowles' Mauve'
Euryops acraeus
Gypsophila repens
Helianthemum 'The Bride'
Helichrysum angustifolium (curry plant)
Iberis umbellata (candytuft)
Ilex (holly hedge)
Jasminum nudiflorum
Lavandula 'Nana Alba'
Lychnis viscaria (sticky Nellie)
Nepeta × *faassenii*
Origanum vulgare 'Aureum'
Parahebe catarractae
Phlox douglasii 'Rosea', *P.*'May Snow'
Prunella × *webbiana* (3), *P.* × *w.*'Loveliness'
Rosa 'New Dawn'
Silene uniflora 'Flore Pleno'
Sisyrinchium striatum
Thymus vulgaris
Veronica austriaca, V.incana, V.prostrata
Viola 'Bowles' Black', *V.cornuta, V.c.alba*

Self-sown violas and pinks throughout

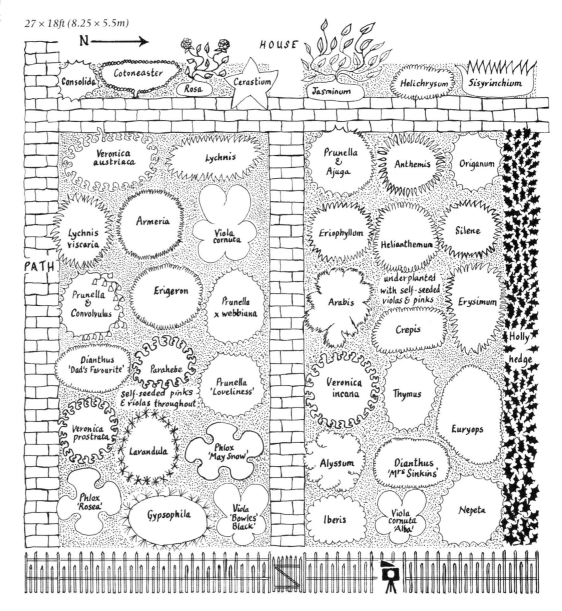

27 × 18ft (8.25 × 5.5m)

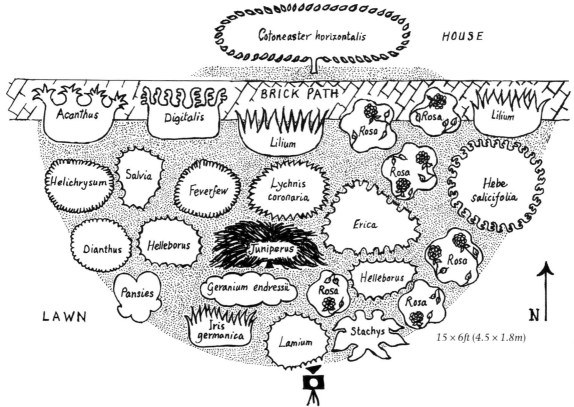

Cotoneaster horizontalis   HOUSE

BRICK PATH

Acanthus   Digitalis   Lilium   Rosa   Rosa   Lilium

Helichrysum   Salvia   Feverfew   Lychnis coronaria   Rosa   Hebe salicifolia

Dianthus   Helleborus   Juniperus   Erica   Rosa

Pansies   Geranium endressii   Rosa   Helleborus   Rosa

LAWN   Iris germanica   Lamium   Stachys   15 × 6ft (4.5 × 1.8m)

N

It is a bold gardener who mixes hot orange with bright scarlet and various shades of pink in his border, but boldness is frequently rewarded in gardens, whereas 'subtle plantings' may end up looking wishy-washy.

Here, a soothing combination of greys, greens, silver and white frames and modifies the impact of the orange tiger-lilies which rise above the magenta flowers of *Lychnis coronaria* and the pink shades of *Geranium endressii* and dianthus.

Hebe salicifolia is a must for anyone wanting to attract butterflies and bees to their garden and who can offer a moderately sheltered site and full sun; in these conditions it grows into a dense dome which, from June to August, is smothered in short white or lilac racemes.

Plant list

Acanthus spinosus
Chrysanthemum parthenium (feverfew)
Cotoneaster horizontalis
Dianthus
Digitalis purpurea alba (white foxgloves)
Erica (white)
Geranium endressii
Hebe salicifolia
Helichrysum italicum
Hellebores (2)
Iris germanica
Juniperus horizontalis
Lamium
Lilium lancifolium (2)
Lychnis coronaria
Pansies
Rosa 'Rosa Mundi' (6)
Salvia (white)
Stachys lanata

Many gardeners are justifiably wary of planting tender or tenderish plants outdoors, even in the most sheltered positions. However, it often seems to be the case that if a youngster can survive its first two or three winters outside it can withstand anything after that. This callistemon is one of the tougher varieties, and has the protection of a south-west-facing Berkshire wall, but, planted over twenty-five years ago, it has had to cope with some pretty severe winters. It rewards its owner's temerity with a display of fiery red 'bottlebrush' flowers throughout the summer, after the deep blue flowers of the *Ceanothus impressus* and the rich pink blooms of the tree peony have faded.

Growing plants up house walls is one of those things that looks innocently undemanding, but turns out to be quite the opposite. How easily the unwary are lured with promises of roses garlanding the windows, wisteria dripping down an entire façade, honeysuckle scrambling over the porch and something 'easy and evergreen' conveniently screening an ugly bit of rendering on the north side. In practice, we learn that gruelling hours in winter and summer must be spent clinging to a ladder with one hand, a pair of secateurs in the other, while the carefully cut lengths of soft twine held between the teeth fall 15 feet to the ground as the first expletive is uttered, usually because a whippy, thorn-encrusted shoot has sprung free and caught the neck, cheek or ear. Of course, this applies only to those shrubs and climbers which require training and fixing to the wall; the self-adhesive type of climber, such as ivies, Virginia creepers and *Hydrangea*

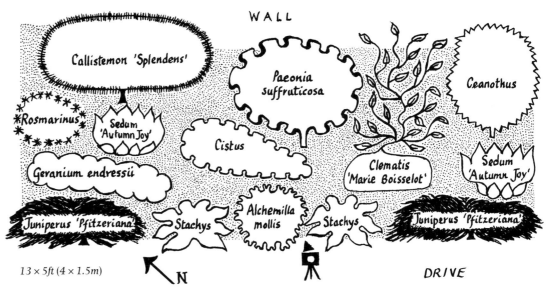

13 × 5ft (4 × 1.5m)

petiolaris, need no such help, but they will have to be kept free of gutters and windows and should only be contemplated if the wall is not in need of painting or pointing.

If labour-intensive, wall-trained shrubs and climbers are out of the question, but a framework of wires is in place, annual climbers such as Canary creeper or *Cobaea scandens* might be considered. Sown from seed, in warmth, early on in the year, these pretty climbers will move fast once planted out and lend their foliage and blooms to the house for a single season.

Plant list

Alchemilla mollis
Callistemon citrinus 'Splendens'
Ceanothus impressus
Cistus × cyprius
Clematis 'Marie Boisselot'
Geranium endressii
Juniperus 'Pfitzeriana'
Paeonia suffruticosa 'Kumagai'
Rosemary
Sedum 'Autumn Joy'
Stachys lanata

A variety of evergreen foliage ensures that this corner of a south Oxfordshire garden is never dull, and a succession of flowers from autumn until early summer makes a cheering sight from the kitchen window.

The scented pink flowers of *Viburnum × bodnantense* appear in October and persist until February. A skirt of autumn-flowering snowdrops (*Galanthus reginae-olgae*) and cyclamen lends support, followed by Christmas roses (*Helleborus niger*). The seed-pods of an elegant grass, *Pennisetum orientale*, also provide interest in the bleakest months of the year.

In spring, a profusion of yellow and white flowers emerges: after the crocuses and daffodils, white columbines and Jacob's ladder (*Polemonium caeruleum* 'Album') mix with bold yellow irises and euphorbias. *Daphne pontica* bears fragrant, spidery blooms in April and May; when these fade, the old-fashioned dianthus 'Charles Musgrave' (single white with a green eye) scents the summer air.

Everyone is familiar with deutzias, but *Deutzia × maliflora* 'Avalanche' is an uncommon and very pretty shrub. In June, scented white flowers weigh down its slender stems; the effect is entirely graceful. *Cotoneaster* 'Exburiensis' is another unusual and slightly less hardy cultivar of a familiar genus. It produces small white flowers in early summer which are followed by clusters of creamy-yellow fruits. It is one of the larger cotoneasters, capable of reaching 15ft (4.5m), with a similar spread; competition for space with the viburnum may be anticipated.

N →

Tulips

Cotoneaster

Polemonium overlapping with earlier Aquilegia (white)

Aquilegia

Iris germanica

Ranunculus gramineus

Ballota 'All Hallows Green'

Helleborus niger

Rosa rublifolia

Euphorbia polychroma

Deutzia × maliflora

Galanthus

Galanthus

Galanthus

Galanthus

underplanted with Cyclamen & Galanthus (both autumn-flowering)

Iris graminea

Viburnum × bodnantense

Hosta ventricosa 'Aureomarginata'

Viola 'Little David'

Daphne pontica

Hosta sieboldiana

Phormium

Geranium Clarkei

Viola 'Little David'

Viola 'Little David'

Dianthus 'Charles Musgrave'

Narcissus poeticus

Hosta 'Aureo Nebulosa'

Crocus 'Snow Bunting'

Alyssum

Primula vulgaris

Thymus 'Silver Queen'

Pennisetum orientale

Dianthus 'Iceberg'

13 × 9ft (4 × 2.75m)

Plant list

Alyssum saxatile citrinum
Ballota 'All Hallows Green'
Cotoneaster 'Exburiensis'
Crocus chrysanthus 'Snow Bunting'
Daphne pontica
Deutzia × maliflora
Dianthus 'Charles Musgrave', D. 'Iceberg'
Euphorbia polychroma
Geranium clarkei 'Kashmir White'
Helleborus niger

Hosta sieboldiana, H. 'Aureo Nebulosa', H. ventricosa
  'Aureomarginata'
Iris germanica (yellow intermediate bearded
  iris) (6)
Iris graminea
Narcissus poeticus
Pennisetum orientale
Phormium 'Dark Delight'
Polemonium caeruleum 'Album'
Primula vulgaris

Ranunculus gramineus
Rosa rubrifolia (R. glauca)
Thymus 'Silver Queen'
Tulipa sprengeri 'Trotter's Form'
Viburnum × bodnantense
Viola 'Little David' (3)

Underplanted with Cyclamen hederifolium
and Galanthus reginae-olgae

Dictionary of Symbols

Abbreviations

bs.	berries
fl., fls.	flower, flowers
fr., frs.	fruit, fruits
ht.	height
incl.	including
lf., lvs.	leaf, leaves
see var.	see variety
sp., spp.	species
spr.	spread

Notes

1. It is not always possible to give sizes for water plants.
2. Small = under 2ft (60cm).
   Very small = under 1ft (30cm).
3. Colour, size and season frequently depend on climate and species/variety. In such cases readers are advised to 'See var.'.

General

ABELIA
Caprifoliaceae
Semi-evergreen wall shrub. White/pink/lilac fls. from late spring to autumn. Size: up to 12 × 8ft (3.5 × 2.5m). See var.

ACACIA
incl. Mimosa, Wattle, Kangaroo thorn, Blackwood, Prickly Moses
Leguminosae
Evergreen tree or shrub acc. to climate. Yellow fls. from winter to spring. Size: up to 40 × 15ft (12 × 4.5m). See var.

ACER
Maple, Sycamore (in Scotland, Plane)
Aceraceae
Deciduous tree. Autumn colour. Size: at maturity up to 50ft (15m). See var.

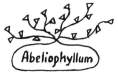

ABELIOPHYLLUM
Oleaceae
Deciduous wall shrub. White/pink fls. in late winter. Size: 4 × 4ft (1.2 × 1.2m).

ACAENA
incl. New Zealand burr
Rosaceae
Evergreen carpeting rock plant. Brown/greeny-red/ scarlet burrs and coloured lvs. in summer. Size: very small.

ACHILLEA
incl. Milfoil, Yarrow, Sneezewort, Sneezeweed
Compositae
Deciduous and evergreen perennial and mat-forming rock plant. Yellow/red/pink/white fls. from late spring. Size: up to 4 × 4ft (1.2 × 1.2m). See var.

ABIES
Fir
Pinaceae
Coniferous tree, erect and prostrate vars. Size: up to 130ft (40m). See var.

ACANTHOPANAX
Araliaceae
Deciduous shrub. Exotic lvs. Size: 6 × 8ft (1.8 × 2.5m).

ACHNATHERUM
incl. Feather/Needle grass
Gramineae
Herbaceous perennial ornamental grass. Size: up to 4 × 2ft (1.2m × 60cm).

ABUTILON
incl. Flowering maple, Chinese lantern
Malvaceae
Deciduous wall shrub. White/pink/orange/ yellow/mauve fls. from late spring to autumn. Size: up to 15 × 12ft (4.5 × 3.5m). See var.

ACANTHUS
incl. Bear's breeches
Acanthaceae
Herbaceous perennial. Mauve/pink/white fls. in late summer. Size: up to 4 × 3ft (1.2m × 90cm).

ACIDANTHERA
incl. Peacock orchid
Iridaceae
Herbaceous corm. White/ reddish-purple fls. in early autumn. Size: up to 3ft (90cm).

ACONITUM
incl. Aconite, Monkshood, Wolfsbane, Helmet flower
Ranunculaceae
Herbaceous perennial. Mainly blue fls. in summer. Size: up to 6ft (1.8m).

ACORUS
incl. Sweet flag
Araceae
Perennial rhizomatous marginal aquatic. Yellow/white fls. Size: up to 3ft (90cm) high. See var.

ACTAEA
incl. Baneberry, Cohosh, Herb Christopher
Ranunculaceae
Herbaceous perennial. White-bluish/yellow fls. from late spring, then bs. Size: up to 3 × 1½ft (90 × 45cm). See var.

ACTINIDIA
incl. Chinese gooseberry, Kiwi fruit, Kolomikta vine
Actinidiaceae
Deciduous woody climber. White fls. early summer. Size: up to 50ft (15m). See var.

ADENOCARPUS
Leguminosae
Deciduous shrub. Yellow fls. in early summer. Size: 10 × 8ft (3 × 2.5m).

ADENOPHORA
Ladybells
Campanulaceae
Herbaceous perennial. Blue/violet-blue fls. in summer. Size: up to 3 × 1½ft (90 × 45cm). See var.

ADIANTUM
Maidenhair fern
Polypodiaceae
Rhizomatous herbaceous fern, some prostrate vars. Size: up to 1½ × 1ft (45 × 30cm). See var.

ADONIS
Ranunculaceae
Dwarf perennial and annual rock plant. Yellow/red fls. in winter, spring and autumn. See var. Size: small.

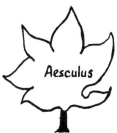

AESCULUS
incl. Horse chestnut, Buckeye
Hippocastanaceae
Deciduous tree. White/pink/red/yellow fls. in late spring. Size: 40 × 33ft (12 × 10m). See var.

AETHIONEMA
Stone-cress
Cruciferae
Evergreen rock plant. Pink fls. in early summer. Size: small.

AGAPANTHUS
African blue lily
Amaryllidaceae
Tuberous deciduous and evergreen plant. Blue/violet/white fls. from late summer to autumn. Size: up to 4 × 2ft (1.2m × 60cm). See var.

AGASTACHE
Mexican giant hyssop
Labiatae
Herbaceous perennial. Pink/crimson fls. from early to mid summer. Size: up to 2 × 1ft (60 × 30cm).

AGAVE
Century plant
Agavaceae (formerly classed in *Amaryllidaceae*)
Evergreen perennial. Greenish-white fls. in summer. Size: up to 20ft (6m). See var.

AJUGA
incl. Bugle, Bugleweed
Labiatae
Sub-shrubby deciduous rock plant. Blue/white/pink fls. in early summer, variously coloured lvs. Size: very small.

ALCHEMILLA
Lady's mantle
Rosaceae
Herbaceous perennial. Greenish-yellow fls. in early summer. Size: small.

AGERATUM
Floss flower
Compositae
Annual. Blue/pink/reddish-mauve fls. in summer. Size: up to 2 × 1½ft (60 × 45cm).

AKEBIA
Lardizabalaceae
Deciduous and evergreen climber. Red/purple/white fls. in spring and winter. Size: up to 40ft (12m). See var.

ALISMA
incl. Water plantain, Mad-dog weed
Alismataceae
Herbaceous perennial marginal aquatic. Pink/creamy-white fls. in summer. Size: small.

AGROSTEMMA
Corn cockle
Caryophyllaceae
Annual. Rosy-lilac fls. in summer. Size: 3 × 1ft (90 × 30cm).

ALBIZIA
incl. Silk tree, Pink siris tree
Leguminosae
Deciduous tree or large shrub. Pink fls. in mid summer. Size: 20 × 20ft (6 × 6m).

ALLIUM
incl. Wild garlic, Prairie onion, Ramsons, Star of Persia
Liliaceae (sometimes classed in *Alliaceae*)
Bulb. Blue/purple/lilac/pink/red/yellow/white fls. from spring to mid summer. Size: up to 5 × 1ft (1.5m × 30cm). See var.

AILANTHUS
Tree of Heaven
Simaroubaceae
Deciduous tree. Size: up to 65ft (20m).

ALCEA
Hollyhock
Malvaceae
Perennial and biennial. Red/pink/purple/yellow/cream/white fls. in summer. Size: up to 9 × 2ft (2.75m × 60cm).

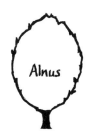

ALNUS
Alder
Betulaceae
Deciduous tree. Size: up to 40 × 18ft (12 × 5.5m).

ALONSOA
Mask flower
Scrophulariaceae
Shrubby perennial and
annual. Orange/red fls.
from summer to autumn.
Size: small.

ALTERNANTHERA
incl. Parrot-leaf, Joseph's
coat, Blood-leaf,
Beefsteak plant
Amaranthaceae
Herbaceous and evergreen
perennial. Bright leaf
colour. Size: small.

× AMARYGIA
Belladonna lily hybrid
Amaryllidaceae
Bulb. Pink/white fls. in
late summer. Size: 2 × 1ft
(60 × 30cm).

ALOPECURUS
Golden foxtail
Gramineae
Ornamental rhizomatous
herbaceous perennial
ground-cover grass. Gold-
striped leaves. Size: small.

ALYSSUM
Cruciferae
Prostrate or trailing sub-
shrub for walls and
rockeries. Yellow/pink/
purple/white fls. in spring
and summer. Size: small.

AMARYLLIS
Belladonna lily
Amaryllidaceae
Bulb. Pink fls. in late
summer. Size: 2 × 1ft
(60 × 30cm).

ALOYSIA (prev. LIPPIA)
Lemon verbena
Verbenaceae
Deciduous shrub or small
tree. Lilac fls. in late
summer. Size: 10 × 10ft
(3 × 3m).

AMARANTHUS
incl. Love-lies-bleeding,
Tassel flower, Joseph's
coat, Green amaranth,
Prince's feather
Amaranthaceae
Annual. Red/green fls. and
coloured lvs. Size: up to
4 × 1½ft (1.2m × 45cm).
See var.

AMELANCHIER
incl. Juneberry,
Serviceberry, Shadbush
Rosaceae
Deciduous tree or shrub.
White fls. and spring leaf
colour, then bs. and
autumn colour. Size: up to
25ft (7.5m). See var.

ALSTROEMERIA
incl. Peruvian/Parrot lily
Alstroemeriaceae
(sometimes classed in
Amaryllidaceae)
Herbaceous perennial.
Yellow/orange/red/pink/
white/purple/mauve fls.
from late spring to
summer. Size: up to 4ft
(1.2m). See var.

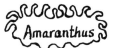

× AMARCRINUM
Crinodonna
Amaryllidaceae
Evergreen bulb. Pink fls.
from late summer to
autumn. Size: up to 3ft
(90cm).

AMPELOPSIS
Vitaceae
Deciduous perennial
woody climber. Orange-
yellow frs. in autumn.
Size: up to 65ft (20m). See
var.

AMSONIA
incl. Periwinkle, Blue
buttons/star, Trailing
myrtle
Apocynaceae
Herbaceous perennial or
sub-shrub. Pink/mauve/
purple/blue/white fls. in
most seasons. Size: up to
3ft (90cm). See var.

ANDROMEDA
incl. Sorrel tree,
Sourwood, Cassiope,
Bog rosemary
Ericaceae
Deciduous tree or shrub
and rock plant. White fls.
in mid summer, scarlet
autumn lvs. Size: up to
40ft (12m). See var.

ANOMATHECA
Lapeirousia
Iridaceae
Herbaceous corm. Red fls.
in mid summer. Size:
small.

ANAGALLIS
Pimpernel, Poor man's
weather-glass
Primulaceae
Prostrate annual. Mainly
blue fls. in summer. Size:
small.

ANDROSACE
Rock jasmine
Primulaceae
Mat-forming alpine. Pink/
white fls. from spring to
late summer. Size: very
small.

ANTENNARIA
Compositae
Evergreen carpeting rock
plant. White/pink/crimson
fls. in late spring. Size: very
small.

ANAPHALIS
Pearly everlasting.
Compositae
Perennial. Yellow/blue-
purple fls. from mid to late
summer. Size: small.

ANEMONE
incl. Windflower, Pasque
flower
Ranunculaceae
Tuberous or rhizomatous
perennial and rock plant.
Pink/white/red/blue/
purple fls. in most seasons.
Size: up to 5 × 2ft
(1.5m × 60cm). See var.

ANTHEMIS
incl. Camomile, Golden
marguerite
Compositae
Evergreen and herbaceous
perennial and annual.
Orange/yellow/white fls.
in early to mid summer.
Size: 2½ × 1½ft (75 ×
45cm).

ANCHUSA
incl. Forget-me-not,
Bugloss, Alkanet
Boraginaceae
Perennial, rock plant and
annual. Blue fls. in early
summer, some repeat in
autumn. Size: small.

ANISODONTEA
Malvaceae
Evergreen shrub and
perennial. Rose-magenta
fls. from spring to autumn.
Size: 3 × 2ft (90 ×
60cm).

ANTHERICUM
incl. Spider plant, St
Bernard's lily
Liliaceae
Rhizomatous evergreen
herbaceous perennial.
White fls. with striped
leaves for summer
bedding. Size: small.

ANTHYLLIS
incl. Hedgehog/Blue
 broom
Leguminosae
Deciduous shrub. Yellow/
orange/violet-blue fls. in
early summer. Size: 2 ×
3ft (60 × 90cm). See var.

ARALIA
incl. Japanese angelica
 tree, Hercules' club,
 Devil's walking stick
Araliaceae
Deciduous tree or shrub.
Creamy white fls. in
autumn. Size: 15 × 15ft
(4.5 × 4.5m).

ARECASTRUM
Queen palm
Palmae
Evergreen palm tree. Size:
up to 25ft (7.5m).

ANTIRRHINUM
incl. Asarina, Snapdragon
Scrophulariaceae
Sub-shrubby perennial
trailing rock plant and
annual. White/orange/
red/yellow/pink fls. in
summer. Size: up to 4 ×
1½ft (1.2m × 45cm). See
var.

ARAUCARIA
incl. Monkey Puzzle, Chile/
 Star/Norfolk Island
 pine, Bunya-bunya
Pinaceae
Coniferous (tropical
evergreen) tree. Size: up to
100ft (30m). See var.

ARENARIA
incl. Sandwort, Irish moss
Caryophyllaceae
Evergreen rock plant.
White/pink fls. from late
spring. Size: very small.

AQUILEGIA
incl. Columbine
Ranunculaceae
Herbaceous perennial and
rock plant. Most colours in
summer. Size: 2½ × 1½ft
(75 × 45cm). See var.

ARBUTUS
incl. Strawberry tree,
 Madrone, Madrona,
 Laurelwood, Oregon
 laurel
Ericaceae
Evergreen tree or shrub.
Whitish fls. in spring then
orange-red frs. Size: up to
25ft (7.5m). See var.

ARGEMONE
incl. Prickly/Mexican/
 Crested poppy, Devil's
 fig
Papaveraceae
Thistly annual. White/
orange/yellow/purple fls.
in summer. Size: up to 4ft
(1.2m).

ARABIS
incl. Rock-cress
Cruciferae
Evergreen rock plant.
White/pink/purple fls. in
spring and summer. Size:
small.

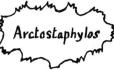

ARCTOSTAPHYLOS
incl. Red bearberry,
 Manzanita,
 Kinnikinnick
Ericaceae
Evergreen small tree or
shrub, some prostrate.
White/deep pink fls. in
spring then deep red frs.
Size: up to 10 × 6ft (3 ×
1.8m).

ARGYRANTHEMUM
 (previously
 CHRYSANTHEMUM)
Compositae
Perennial, evergreen sub-
shrubby rock plant and
annual. Red/pink/yellow/
white fls. in most seasons.
Size: up to 6 × 1½ft
(1.8m × 45cm). See var.

ARISAEMA
incl. Green dragon, Cobra
lily, Jack-in-the-pulpit
Araceae
Tuberous perennial.
Colour in spathes and frs.
from spring to late
summer. Size: up to 3ft
(90cm). See var.

ARMERIA
Thrift
Plumbaginaceae
Evergreen tufty perennial
and rock plant. Pink/white
fls. from late spring to
summer. Size: up to 2 ×
1ft (60 × 30cm). See var.

ARTEMISIA
incl. Southernwood, Lad's
love, Wormwood, Old
man/woman, Absinthe
Compositae
Evergreen and deciduous
shrub, perennial and rock
plant. Yellow/white fls. in
summer or autumn. Size:
up to 7 × 6ft (2 × 1.8m).
See var.

ARISARUM
Mouse plant
Araceae
Rhizomatous perennial
rock plant. Size: small.

ARNICA
Mountain tobacco
Compositae
Alpine and border
perennial. Orange-yellow
fls. in early summer. Size:
small.

ARUM
incl. Sweet flag, Bog or
Water arum, Golden
club
Araceae
Rhizomatous marginal
aquatic. Spear-shaped lvs.
in autumn and early
winter. Size: up to 3ft
(90cm). See var.

ARISTOLOCHIA
Dutchman's pipe
Aristolochiaceae
Evergreen twining
climber. Yellowish-brown
fls. in early summer. Size:
up to 30ft (9m). See var.

ARONIA
Chokeberry
Rosaceae
Deciduous shrub. Autumn
colour. Size: up to 7 × 7ft
(2 × 2m).

ARUNCUS
Goat's beard
Rosaceae
White fls. in early
summer, then seeds. Size:
up to 7 × 4ft (2 × 1.2m).

ARISTOTELIA
Elaeocarpaceae
Evergreen shrub and
deciduous tree. Foliage.
Size: up to 10 × 15ft (3 ×
4.5m).

ARRHENATHERUM
Variegated oat grass
Gramineae
Ornamental herbaceous
grass. Size: 2 × 1ft (60 ×
30cm).

ARUNDINARIA
Bamboo
Gramineae
Woody-stemmed
evergreen or semi-
evergreen perennial giant
grass. Size: up to 15ft
(4.5m). See var.

ASARINA
Scrophulariaceae
Trailing perennial rock plant, and in USA also annual vine to 10ft (3m). Whitish-pink/yellow fls. all summer. Size: very small.

ASPARAGUS
Asparagus fern incl. Glory lily (also see vegetables, p. 156)
Liliaceae
Evergreen and deciduous tuberous perennial. Red to yellow fls. all summer, some vars. frs. Size: up to 10ft (3m). See var.

ASTELIA
Liliaceae
Evergreen clump-forming perennial. Grassy lvs. and inconspicuous fls. Size: 2 × 5ft (60cm × 1.5m).

ASARUM
Wild ginger
Aristolochiaceae
Rhizomatous mostly evergreen ground-cover. Size: small.

ASPERULA
Woodruff
Rubiaceae
Herbaceous perennial ground-cover and annual. Pink/blue fls. in early summer. Size: $1\frac{1}{2} \times 1\frac{1}{2}$ft (45 × 45cm).

ASTER
incl. Michaelmas daisies
Compositae
Herbaceous perennial, clumpy alpine and biennial. Fls. in almost all colours from late summer to autumn. Size: up to 4ft (1.2m). See var.

ASCLEPIAS
incl. Milkweed, Blood-flower, Swamp milkweed, Butterfly-weed, Pleurisy root
Asclepiadaceae
Herbaceous perennial. Pink/crimson/orange fls. in summer. Size: up to 4 × 2ft (1.2m × 60cm). See var.

ASPHODELINE, ASPHODELUS
incl. Jacob's rod, Yellow asphodel, King's spear
Liliaceae
Rhizomatous and tuberous herbaceous perennial. Yellow/white fls. in late spring. Size: up to 4 × 1ft (1.2m × 30cm). See var.

ASTILBE
Saxifragaceae
Herbaceous perennial, ground-cover. White/pink/red/purple fls. in summer. Size: up to 4ft (1.2m). See var.

ASIMINA
American paw-paw
Annonaceae
Deciduous shrub or small tree. Purple fls. in spring, autumn colour and frs. Size: up to 12 × 7ft (3.5 × 2m).

ASPLENIUM
Spleenwort
Polypodiaceae
Evergreen fern. Size: small.

ASTILBOIDES
Rodgersia
Saxifragaceae
Creamy-white fls. in early to mid summer. Size: 3 × $2\frac{1}{2}$ft (90 × 75cm).

ASTRANTIA
Masterwort
Umbelliferae
Herbaceous perennial.
Pink/white/purple-red fls.
in summer. Size: up to 3 ×
1ft (90 × 30cm).

AUCUBA
incl. Madwort, Basket of
gold, Spotted laurel,
Gold-dust plant
Cornaceae
Evergreen bushy shrub.
Scarlet bs. Size: 10 × 10ft
(3 × 3m).

AZARA
Flacourtiaceae
Evergreen shrub or small
tree. Yellow fls. early
spring then bs. Size: up to
16 × 10ft (5 × 3m). See
var.

ATHYRIUM
incl. Glade fern, Lady fern,
Japanese painted fern,
Silvery spleenwort
Polypodiaceae
Evergreen fern. Size: up to
3 × 2ft (90 × 60cm), also
dwarfs. See var.

AURICULA
Primula
Primulaceae
Clump-forming alpine,
border and show
perennial. Primula fls.,
many colours, in summer.
Size: small.

AZOLLA
Fairy moss
Azolliaceae
Floating aquatic. Leaf
colour. Size: very small.

ATRIPLEX
incl. Tree purslane, Orach,
Red mountain/French
spinach, Ruby chard
Chenopodiaceae
Evergreen silver shrub and
annual. Blood-red lvs. Size:
up to 6 × 7ft (1.8 × 2m).
See var.

AURINIA
incl. Gold dust
Cruciferae
Evergreen mat-forming
rock plant. Yellow fls. in
spring. Size: small.

BABIANA
Baboon flower
Iridaceae
Herbaceous corm. Blue/
white/violet/reddish-
mauve fls. in spring. Size:
small.

AUBRIETA
incl. False rock cress
Cruciferae
Evergreen trailing, mat-
forming rock plant. Pink/
red/purple-blue fls. in
early summer. Size: small.

AZALEA *see*
RHODODENDRON

BACCHARIS
incl. Coyote bush,
Chaparral broom,
Groundsel bush
Compositae
Evergreen spreading/
ground-cover shrub.
Whitish seed-heads. Size:
up to 2 × 6ft (60cm ×
1.8m). See var.

BALDELLIA
Alismataceae
Evergreen and deciduous perennial bog or submerged water plant. Pink/white fls. in summer. Size: very small.

BEGONIA
Begoniaceae
Rhizomatous and tuberous evergreen and deciduous shrub, perennial and annual. Wide variety of colours except blue and mauve in most seasons. Size: up to $3\frac{1}{2}$ft (1.1m). See var.

BERBERIS
Barberry
Berberidaceae
Evergreen and deciduous shrub. Yellow fls., bs. and autumn colour. Size: up to 10×10ft (3×3m). See var.

BALLOTA
Horehound
Labiatae
Sprawling herbaceous perennial. Mauve fls. in summer. Size: 2×2ft (60×60cm).

BELAMCANDA
incl. Blackberry lily, Leopard flower
Iridaceae
Rhizomatous herbaceous plant. Pink/orange/blue/purple/yellow/red fls. all summer. Size: up to 3ft (90cm).

BERGENIA
Saxifragaceae
Semi-evergreen perennial ground-cover. White/red/purple fls. from early spring. Size: up to 2ft (60cm).

BANKSIA
Australian honeysuckle
Proteaceae
Evergreen tree or shrub. Red/purple/yellow fls. in autumn and winter. Size: up to 40ft (12m). See var.

BELLIS
Common European/ English daisy
Compositae
Annual. White/pink/yellow fls. in spring and summer. Size: very small.

BESSERA
Coral drops
Amaryllidaceae
Corms. Variously tinted white fls. in summer. Size: up to 3ft (90cm).

BAPTISIA
incl. False/Wild indigo, Horsefly
Leguminosae
Herbaceous perennial. Blue/yellow fls. in early summer. Size: 4×2ft (1.2m $\times$ 60cm).

BERBERIDOPSIS
Coral plant
Flacourtiaceae
Evergreen scrambling, twining wall shrub. Red fls. in late summer. Size: up to 5–10ft (1.5–3m).

BETULA
Birch
Betulaceae
Deciduous tree with peeling bark and catkins. Size: up to 36×20ft (11×6m). See var.

BIDENS
Compositae
Annual. Yellow fls. in summer and autumn. Size: small.

BRACHYCOME
Swan River daisy
Compositae
Annual. Blue/pink/white fls. in summer and autumn. Size: small.

BRIZA
Quaking grass
Gramineae
Ornamental perennial grass. Size: 2 × 1ft (60 × 30cm).

BLECHNUM
Hard fern, Deer fern
Polypodiaceae
Evergreen perennial fern, some creeping. Size: up to 2 × 1ft (60 × 30cm), also dwarf.

BRACHYGLOTTIS
Compositae
Evergreen shrub. White fls. (some vars. purple leaves) in early spring. Size: up to 15 × 15ft (4.5 × 4.5m). See var.

BROUSSONETIA
incl. Paper mulberry
Moraceae
Deciduous tree or shrub. Catkins. Size: 30 × 25ft (9 × 7.5m).

BOCCONIA *see* **MACLEAYA**

BRASSICA
Ornamental or flowering kale and cabbage
Cruciferae
Annual and biennial ornamental vegetables. Variegated white, pink, purple in summer, autumn and winter. Size: small.

BROWALLIA
Solanaceae
Annual. Blue/white fls. all summer. Size: small.

BOUTELOUA
incl. Blue grama, Mosquito Grass
Gramineae
Ornamental perennial grass. Size: under 2ft (60cm).

BRIMEURA
Spanish hyacinth
Liliaceae
Bulb. Blue/white fls. in late spring. Size: very small.

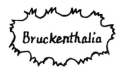

BRUCKENTHALIA
Spike heath
Ericaceae
Evergreen sprawling rock plant. Pink fls. in early summer. Size: small.

BRUNNERA
Siberian bugloss
Boraginaceae
Perennial and ground-cover. Blue fls. in early summer. Size: small.

BUTIA
Pindo/Jelly palm
Palmae
Evergreen palm tree. Size: up to 15ft (4.5m).

CALCEOLARIA
Scrophulariaceae
Evergreen perennial, sub-shrub, climber, annual and biennial. Yellow-red fls. in summer. Size: up to 2 × 1ft (60 × 30cm). See var.

BUDDLEJA
Butterfly bush, Summer lilac, Orange ball tree
Loganiaceae
Deciduous shrub. Mauve/purple/red/white/orange/yellow fls. in summer and autumn. Size: up to 25 × 12ft (7.5 × 3.5m). See var.

BUTOMUS
Flowering rush
Butomaceae
Rhizomatous marginal aquatic. Pink fls., purple lvs. Size: up to 4ft (1.2m).

CALENDULA
Marigold
Compositae
Annual. Cream/yellow/orange fls. from spring to autumn. Size: 2 × 1½ft (60 × 45cm).

BUPHTHALMUM
Yellow/Willow-leaf ox-eye
Compositae
Perennial. Yellow fls. in summer. Size: 2 × 2ft (60 × 60cm).

or

BUXUS
Box
Buxaceae
Evergreen shrub for hedging, topiary, also small tree. Size: up to 10 × 10ft (3 × 3m). See var.

CALLA
Bog/Water arum
Araceae
Deciduous or semi-evergreen marginal aquatic. White spathes, red frs. in summer. Size: ht. very small.

BUPLEURUM
incl. Hare's ear
Umbelliferae
Semi-evergreen, evergreen shrub and herbaceous perennial. Yellow fls. in summer and autumn. Size: up to 7 × 7ft (2 × 2m). See var.

CAESALPINA
Barbados pride, Bird of paradise shrub
Leguminosae
Deciduous or evergreen wall shrub or small tree. Yellow fls. from mid to late summer. Size: up to 30ft (9m). See var.

CALLICARPA
Beauty-berry, French mulberry
Verbenaceae
Deciduous shrub. Pink/purple fls. then lilac or white frs. and autumn colour. Size: 8 × 5ft (2.5 × 1.5m).

CALLISTEMON
Bottlebrush
Myrtaceae
Evergreen shrub. Scarlet/
crimson/pink/white/
cream fls. in summer. Size:
up to 30 × 15ft (9 ×
4.5m). See var.

CALOCHORTUS
incl. Cat's ears, Fairy
lantern, Mariposa lily,
Butterfly/Star/Globe
tulip, Beavertail grass
Liliaceae
Corm. White/cream/
yellow/orange/red/pink/
lilac/purple fls. in spring
and summer. Size: up to
2ft (60cm).

CAMELLIA
Theaceae
Evergreen shrub and tree.
White/pink/red fls. in late
winter and spring. Size: up
to 12 × 12ft (3.5 ×
3.5m). See var.

CALLISTEPHUS
China aster
Compositae
Annual. White/pink/red/
purple/blue fls. from
summer to autumn. Size:
up to 2ft (60cm).

CALTHA
incl. Marsh marigold,
Kingcup, Water cowslip
Ranunculaceae
Deciduous perennial
marginal aquatic. Yellow/
white fls. in late winter
and spring. Size: up to 3ft
(90cm). See var.

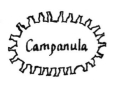

CAMPANULA
Bellflower, Canterbury/
Coventry bells, Venus's
looking-glass, Fairy's
thimble, Harebell
Campanulaceae
Herbaceous perennial,
rock plant and annual.
White/pink/blue fls. in
summer. Size: up to 3 ×
2ft (90 × 60cm). See var.

CALLUNA
incl. Ling, Scotch heather,
Carolina allspice,
Common sweet-shrub
Ericaceae
Evergreen, low-growing
bushy shrub. Red/purple/
pink/white fls. from
summer to autumn. Size:
up to 2 × 2½ft (60 ×
75cm). See var.

CALYCANTHUS
incl. Carolina allspice,
Sweetshrub
Calycanthaceae
Deciduous shrub. Red-
purple fls. in summer. Size:
8 × 8ft (2.5 × 2.5m).

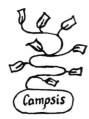

CAMPSIS
incl. Trumpet creeper/
honeysuckle, American/
Chinese trumpet vine
Bignoniaceae
Deciduous, woody,
twining climber. Yellow/
orange/red fls. in late
summer. Size: up to 40ft
(12m).

CALOCEDRUS
Incense cedar
Cupressaceae
Coniferous tree: columnar
or conical. Size: at
maturity over 80ft (25m).

CAMASSIA
Camass, Quamash, Wild
hyacinth
Liliaceae
Bulb. White/violet/blue fls.
in late spring. Size: up to
4ft (1.2m). See var.

CANNA
incl. Indian shot
Cannaceae
Rhizomatous perennial.
Red/orange/pink/yelow/
white fls. from summer to
autumn. Size: up to 5ft
(1.5m). See var.

CARAGANA
Pea tree/shrub
Leguminosae
Deciduous shrub, erect, prostrate or weeping. Yellow fls. in spring and early summer. Size: up to 20 × 12ft (6 × 3.5m). See var.

CARLINA
Stemless thistle
Compositae
Evergreen rock plant. Whitish fls. in summer. Size: very small.

CARYA
Hickory
Juglandaceae
Deciduous tree. Autumn colour and nuts. Size: up to 30 × 18ft (9 × 5.5m). See var.

CARDAMINE
Bitter/Meadow cress, Lady's smock, Cuckoo flower
Cruciferae
Herbaceous perennial. White/pink/lilac/purple fls. in spring. Size: small.

CARMICHAELIA
Leguminosae
Deciduous shrub, erect or hummock-forming rock plant. Violet-purple fls. in early summer. Size: up to 6 × 5ft (1.8 × 1.5m). See var.

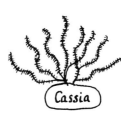

CARYOPTERIS
Bluebeard
Verbenaceae
Deciduous sub-shrub. Blue fls. from late summer to autumn. Size: up to 3 × 4ft (90cm × 1.2m). See var.

CARDIOCRINUM
Giant lily
Liliaceae
Bulb. Creamy-white fls. in summer. Size: up to 8ft (2.5m).

CARPENTARIA
Tree anemone
Hydrangaceae
Evergreen shrub. White fls. in mid summer. Size: 6 × 6ft (1.8 × 1.8m).

CASSIA
incl. Senna, Golden shower, Indian laburnum, Pudding pipe-tree
Leguminosae
Evergreen and deciduous tree, shrub, perennial and annual. Yellow fls. Season and size vary greatly. See var.

CAREX
Sedge
Cyperaceae
Evergreen grassy perennial. Size: up to 4 × 3ft (1.2m × 90cm).

CARPINUS
Hornbeam
Betulaceae
Deciduous columnar or conical tree. Catkins and autumn colour. Size: up to 30 × 15ft (9 × 4.5m). See var.

CASSIOPE
Ericaceae
Evergreen, low-growing shrubby rock plant. White fls. in spring. Size: small.

CASTANEA
Chestnut
Fagaceae
Deciduous tree with edible nuts. Size: at maturity 50 × 40ft (15 × 12m).

CEANOTHUS
incl. Blue-blossom, Californian lilac, Carmel creeper
Rhamnaceae
Evergreen and deciduous shrub and small tree. Blue (rarely pink) fls. in spring to autumn. Size: up to 20 × 20ft (6 × 6m). See var.

CELOSIA
Amaranthaceae
Annual. Red/orange/ yellow fls. from summer to autumn. Size: up to 2 × 1ft (60 × 30cm).

CATALPA
Catawba, Indian bean tree
Bignoniaceae
Deciduous tree. White fls. in late summer. Size: up to 25 × 25ft (7.5 × 7.5m). See var.

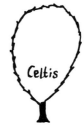

CEDRUS
Cedar
Pinaceae
Evergreen coniferous tree: vars. incl. tall, conical, flat-topped, pendulous, bushy, prostrate and dwarf. Size: at maturity up to 100ft (30m). See var.

CELTIS
incl. Nettle tree, Hackberry, Sugarberry
Ulmaceae
Deciduous tree. Size: at maturity up to 60ft (18m). See var.

CATANANCHE
Cupid's dart, Blue cupidone, Blue succory
Compositae
Perennial. Blue/white fls. from mid to late summer. Size: 2½ × 1½ft (75 × 45cm).

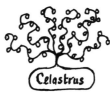

CELASTRUS
Climbing bittersweet, Staff vine
Celastraceae
Deciduous twining climber. Red seeds. Size: up to 50 × 40ft (15 × 12m). See var.

CENTAUREA
incl. Knapweed, Cornflower, Mountain bluet, Basket flower, Sweet sultan
Compositae
Thistly perennial, annual and rock plant. Pink/blue/ yellow/red/purple fls., for season see var. Size: up to 6ft (1.8m). See var.

CAUTLEYA
Zingiberaceae
Rhizomatous perennial. Yellow fls. in late summer. Size: 2 × 1½ft (60 × 45cm).

CELMISIA
Compositae
Evergreen mat-forming perennial rock plant. White fls. in mid summer. Size: small.

CENTRANTHUS
Red valerian
Valerianaceae
Herbaceous perennial. Crimson/white fls. during long summer season. Size: 2 × 3ft (60 × 90cm).

CEPHALARIA
Giant/Yellow scabious
Dipsacaceae
Herbaceous perennial.
Yellow fls. in summer.
Size: 6 × 4ft (1.8 ×
1.2m).

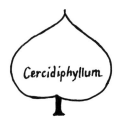

CERCIDIPHYLLUM
Katsura tree
Cercidiphyllaceae
Deciduous tree. Autumn
colour. Size: at maturity to
65ft (20m).

CHAENOMELES
Flowering and common
   quince
Rosaceae
Deciduous shrub and tree.
Red/pink/white fls. in
winter and spring; frs.
Size: up to 15 × 12ft
(4.5 × 3.5m). See var.

CEPHALOTAXUS
incl. Plum yew, Cow's tail
   pine
Cephalotaxaceae
Evergreen coniferous
shrub or small shrubby,
spreading or columnar
tree. Size: 10 × 10ft (3 ×
3m). See var.

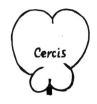

CERCIS
incl. Judas tree, Redbud
Leguminosae
Deciduous shrub and tree.
Pink/white/purple fls. Size:
up to 30 × 20ft (9 × 6m).
See var.

CHAMAECYPARIS
incl. False cypress,
   Lawson's cypress, Port
   Orford cedar
Cupressaceae
Evergreen coniferous tree,
conical or columnar, also
dwarf, spreading shrub.
Size: up to 100ft (30m).
See var.

CERASTIUM
incl. Alpine mouse-ear,
   Snow-in-summer
Carophyllaceae
Perennial and annual,
some vars. ground-cover.
White fls. in summer. Size:
very small.

CESTRUM
incl. Night jessamine
Solanaceae
Evergreen semi-climbing
shrub. Orange/purple/
crimson/cream-white/
yellow-green fls. in
summer, then bs. Size: up
to 10 × 7ft (3 × 2m).

CHEIRANTHUS
(see also ERYSIMUM)
Wallflower
Cruciferae
Evergreen, semi-evergreen
sub-shrub, perennial and
rock plant. Cream/yellow/
orange fls. in spring and
summer. Size: up to 2½ ×
1½ft (75 × 45cm). See
var.

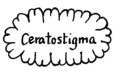

CERATOSTIGMA
Chinese plumbago
Plumbaginaceae
Evergreen and deciduous
shrub and perennial. Blue
fls. in summer then
autumn colour. Size: up to
4 × 5ft (1.2 × 1.5m). See
var.

CETERACH
incl. Spleenwort, Rusty-
   back fern
Polypodiaceae
Perennial, herbaceous
fern. Size: very small.

CHELONE
Turtle-head
Scrophulariaceae
Perennial. Pink fls. from
late summer to autumn.
Size: small.

CHIMONANTHUS
Wintersweet
Calycanthaceae
Deciduous shrub. Yellow
fls. from winter to early
spring. Size: 8 × 8ft
(2.5 × 2.5m).

CHIONANTHUS
incl. Fringe tree, Old man's
beard
Oleaceae
Deciduous shrub. White
fls. in early summer. Size:
12 × 12ft (3.5 × 3.5m).

CHIONODOXA
Glory of the snow
Liliaceae
Bulb, alpine. Blue/pink fls.
in early spring. Size: very
small.

CHLIDANTHUS
incl. Perfumed fairy/
Delicate lily
Amaryllidaceae
Bulbous rock plant. Yellow
fls. in early summer. Size:
small.

CHOISYA
Mexican orange
Rutaceae
Evergreen shrub. White
fls. in late spring. Size: 7 ×
8ft (2 × 2.5m).

CHORDOSPARTIUM
Leguminosae
Almost leafless shrub or
tree. Lilac fls. in early
summer. Size: 15 × 12ft
(4.5 × 3.5m).

CHRYSANTHEMUM
incl. Paris/Shasta/Moon/
Ox-eye daisy, Feverfew,
Pyrethrum, Marguerite
Compositae
Evergreen sub-shrubby
rock plant, perennial and
annual. Red/pink/yellow/
white fls. most seasons.
Size: up to 6 × 1½ft
(1.8m × 45cm). See var.

CHRYSOGONUM
Compositae
Herbaceous perennial.
Yellow fls. from spring to
autumn. Size: small.

CICHORIUM
incl. Chicory, Wild
succory, Belgian/French
endive
Compositae
Vegetable usable as
decorative border plant.
Blue/pink/white fls. from
late summer to autumn.
Size: 5 × 2ft (1.5m ×
60cm).

CIMICIFUGA
incl. Bugbane, Black
snake-root
Ranunculaceae
Perennial. Creamy-white/
greenish-yellow/white fls.
in early autumn. Size: up
to 7ft (2m). See var.

CINERARIA
Compositae
Sub-shrubby perennial or
annual. Silvery-white
leaves and yellow/pink/
purple/blue fls. in winter,
spring or summer. Size:
small.

CIRSIUM
Ornamental thistle
Compositae
Herbaceous perennial.
Purple fls. in mid summer.
Size: 4 × 2ft (1.2m ×
60cm).

CISTUS
Rock rose, Sun rose
Cistaceae
Evergreen shrub. White/
pink/lilac fls. from late
spring to mid summer.
Size: up to 6 × 6ft (1.8 ×
1.8m). See var.

CLARKIA
Onagraceae
Annual. White/pink/red/
lavender fls. from mid to
late summer. Size: up to
2 × 1ft (60 × 30cm).

CLETHRA
Summer-sweet, Sweet
    pepper bush, Lily-of-the-
    valley tree
Clethraceae
Deciduous shrub or small
tree. Creamy-white/pink
fls. from mid to late
summer: autumn colour.
Size: up to 25 × 20ft
(7.5 × 6m). See var.

CITRUS
incl. Orange, Lemon,
    Mandarin, Tangerine,
    Satsuma, Calamondin
Rutaceae
Evergreen tree and shrub:
conservatory plants in UK.
White fls. spring to early
summer then frs. Size: see
var.

CLEMATIS
Old man's beard,
    Traveller's joy
Ranunculaceae
Deciduous and evergreen
twining climber and
herbaceous perennial.
Wide range of colours,
seasons and sizes. See var.

CLEYERA
Theaceae
Evergreen shrub. White
fls. early to mid summer.
Size: up to 8 × 10ft
(2.5 × 3m).

CLADANTHUS
Palm Springs daisy
Compositae
Annual. Yellow fls. in
summer and autumn. Size:
2½ × 1ft (75 × 30cm).

CLEOME
Spider flower
Capparaceae
Annual. White/pink/
purple fls. from mid
summer. Size: 4 × 1½ft
(1.2m × 45cm).

CLIANTHUS
incl. Sturt's desert pea,
    Glory pea, Parrot's bill,
    Lobster claw
Leguminosae
Evergreen or semi-
evergreen sprawling
shrub. Reddish-purple/
white fls. in early summer.
Size: 4 × 4ft (1.2 ×
1.2m).

CLADASTRIS
incl. Yellowwood, Virgilia
Leguminosae
Deciduous tree. White fls.
and autumn colour. Size:
30 × 30ft (9 × 9m).

CLERODENDRON
Glory-bower
Verbenaceae
Deciduous shrub or small
tree. Purplish-red/white/
blue fls. in late summer
and autumn. Size: up to
12 × 15ft (3.5 × 4.5m).
See var.

CLINTONIA
Bluebeard lily
Liliaceae
Herbaceous rhizomatous
perennial. Pink/yellow/
white fls. in late spring,
early summer, then blue
or black bs. Size: up to 2 ×
1ft (60 × 30cm).

COBAEA
incl. Cathedral/Monastery
  bells, Cup-and-saucer
  vine, Mexican ivy
Polemoniaceae
Annual tendrilled climber.
Purple/white fls. all
summer. Size: up to 20ft
(6m).

COLLETIA
Rhamnaceae
Deciduous shrub. White/
pink/yellow fls. in
autumn. Size: up to 8 ×
7ft (2.5 × 2m).

COLUTEA
Bladder senna
Leguminosae
Deciduous shrub. Yellow-
red fls. in summer then frs.
Size: 6 × 8ft (1.8 ×
2.5m).

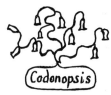

CODONOPSIS
Bonnet bellflower
Campanulaceae
Herbaceous woody
climber and sprawling var.
for rock gardens. Blue fls.
in summer. Size: up to 6ft
(1.8m).

COLLINSIA
incl. Chinese houses
Scrophulariaceae
Annual. White/lilac fls. all
summer. Size: up to 2ft
(60cm).

CONSOLIDA
incl. Larkspur, Annual
  delphinium
Ranunculaceae
Annual. Blue/purple/pink/
white fls. in early to mid
summer. Size: up to 4 ×
1ft (1.2m × 30cm). See
var.

COIX
Job's tears
Gramineae
Ornamental annual wild
grass. Size: 3 × 1ft (90 ×
30cm) or more.

COLOCASIA
incl. Elephant's ear,
  Egyptian taro
Araceae
Deciduous or evergreen
perennial tuberous
marginal aquatic. Foliage
and edible tubers. Size:
6 × 6ft (1.8 × 1.8m).

CONVALLARIA
Lily of the valley
Liliaceae
Rhizomatous woodland
plant. White/pink fls. in
late spring. Size: very
small.

COLCHICUM
Autumn crocus, Meadow
  saffron
Liliaceae
Corm. White/lilac/purple/
pink/red/yellow fls. in
spring and autumn. Size:
small.

COLQUHOUNIA
Labiatae
Evergreen straggly shrub.
Orange-red fls. in late
summer and autumn. Size:
up to 10 × 8ft (3 ×
2.5m).

CONVOLVULUS
incl. Morning glory,
  Bindweed
Convolvulaceae
Evergreen shrub, climbing,
bushy sub-shrub, dwarf
perennial and annual.
Pink/purple/white/red/
blue fls. in summer. Size:
up to 8ft (2.5m). See var.

CORDYLINE
incl. Cabbage tree, Red
palm lily, Dracaena,
Grass palm
Agavaceae
Evergreen shrub and tree.
Size: up to 12 × 8ft
(3.5 × 2.5m).

CORONILLA
Scorpion senna
Leguminosae
Deciduous or evergreen
shrub and perennial.
Yellow fls. from spring to
autumn. Size: up to 10 ×
10ft (3 × 3m).

CORYLOPSIS
Winter hazel
Hamamelidaceae
Deciduous spreading
shrub. Yellow fls. in
spring. Size: up to 10 ×
8ft (3 × 2.5m).

COREOPSIS
Tickseed
Compositae
Herbaceous perennial.
Yellow/orange fls. all
summer. Size: up to 2 ×
1½ft (60 × 45cm).

CORTADERIA
Pampas grass
Gramineae
Evergreen or herbaceous
ornamental grass. Size: up
to 12ft (3.5m). See var.

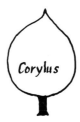

CORYLUS
Hazel, Cobnut, Filbert
Corylaceae
Deciduous tree, mostly
shrubby, also twisted or
weeping. Catkins, nuts.
Size: up to 25 × 15ft
(7.5 × 4.5m). See var.

CORNUS
incl. Dogwood, Cornel,
Bunchberry
Cornaceae
Deciduous and evergreen
tree and shrub, and
rhizomatous perennial.
Whitish fls. in spring to
early summer; bs.; stem
colour. Size: up to 20 ×
18ft (6 × 5.5m). See var.

CORTUSA
Primulaceae
Perennial rock plant.
Pink/white fls. in spring
and summer. Size: small.

COSMOS
Cosmea
Compositae
Tuberous perennial and
annual. Red/yellow/pink/
white and mixed colour fls.
in summer and early
autumn. Size: 4 × 2ft
(1.2m × 60cm). See var.

COROKIA
incl. Wire-netting bush
Cornaceae
Evergreen shrub. Yellow
fls. in late spring. Size: up
to 5 × 6ft (1.5 × 1.8m).

CORYDALIS
Fumariaceae
Tuberous or rhizomatous
annual, herbaceous rock
plant. Yellow/blue/purple/
white/red fls. from late
spring to summer. Size:
small.

COTINUS
incl. Smoke tree/bush,
Venetian sumach,
Chittam wood
Anacardiaceae
Deciduous shrub and tree.
Purple fls. in summer
turning to 'smoke', then
autumn colour. Size: up to
30 × 15ft (9 × 4.5m).
See var.

COTONEASTER
Rosaceae
Evergreen, semi-evergreen and deciduous shrub and tree: tall, bushy, arching or prostrate. White/pink fls. in early summer; bs. and some vars. autumn colour. Size: see var.

CRATAEGUS
incl. Hawthorn, May,
  Quickthorn
Rosaceae
Deciduous tree and shrub. White/pink/crimson fls. in late spring: frs. (haws) and autumn colour. Size: up to 25 × 20ft (7.5 × 6m). See var.

CROCOSMIA
Montbretia
Iridaceae
Semi-evergreen corm. Yellow/red/orange fls. in summer. Size: up to 4 × 1ft (1.2m × 30cm). See var.

COTULA
incl. Brass buttons,
  Pincushion plant
Compositae
Evergreen carpeting rock plants, annual and marginal aquatic. Yellow/red-black fls. in summer. Size: very small.

CREPIS
Hawkweed
Compositae
Rock plant and annual. Orange/pink/white fls. in summer. Size: very small.

CROCUS
Iridaceae
Corm. Many colours in late winter, early spring, also autumn. See var. Size: very small.

CRAMBE
Cruciferae
Herbaceous perennial. White fls. in summer. Size: 6 × 4ft (1.8 × 1.2m).

CRINODENDRON
incl. Lantern tree
Elaeocarpaceae
Evergreen shrub. Crimson/white fls. in spring and late summer. See var. Size: up to 9 × 7ft (2.75 × 2m).

CRYPTOGRAMMA
Parsley fern
Polypodiaceae
Herbaceous perennial fern. Size: very small.

CRASSULA
Crassulaceae
Evergreen rock plant. Crimson/white/pink/fls. in summer. Size: very small.

CRINUM
Amaryllidaceae
Bulb. White/pink fls. in late summer. Size: up to 4 × 3ft (1.2m × 90cm). See var.

CRYPTOMERIA
Japanese cedar
Taxodiaceae
Coniferous conical, columnar or pendulous tree: bushy shrub: dwarf, pyramidal, compact, prostrate rock plant. Some vars. autumn colour. Size: up to 40 × 16ft (12 × 5m). See var.

CUCURBITA
Ornamental gourd
Cucurbitaceae
Annual tendrilled climber.
Yellow fls. then green/
yellow/orange frs. Size:
10–20ft (3–6m).

CUPRESSUS
True cypress
Cupressaceae
Coniferous tree: conical,
pyramidal, compact,
columnar, pendulous,
dense, spreading and
dwarf. Size: See var.

CYMBALARIA
Dwarf Kenilworth ivy, Ivy-
leaved toadflax
Scrophulariaceae
Evergreen perennial rock
plant. Pink/blue/purple/
white fls. all summer. Size:
small.

CUNNINGHAMIA
Chinese fir
Taxodiaceae
Coniferous tree. Size: 30 ×
15ft (9 × 4.5m).

CYANANTHUS
Trailing bellflower
Campanulaceae
Prostrate, mat-forming
rock plant. Blue fls. from
late summer. Size: very
small.

CYNARA
Globe artichoke
Compositae
Vegetable grown as border
plant. Mauve fls. in mid
summer. Size: up to 5 ×
5ft (1.5 × 1.5m).

CUPHEA
incl. Loosestrife, Cigar
    flower, Firecracker plant
Lythraceae
Evergreen sub-shrub. Red
fls. in summer. Size: 1 ×
1ft (30 × 30cm).

CYCLAMEN
Primulaceae
Tuberous perennial, some
evergreen. White/pink/
red/purple fls. in all
seasons: see var. Size: very
small.

CYNOGLOSSUM
Hound's-tongue, Chinese
    forget-me-not
Boraginaceae
Perennial and annual.
Blue fls. in early to mid
summer. Size: up to 3 ×
1ft (90 × 30cm).

× CUPRESSOCYPARIS
Leyland cypress
Cupressaceae
Evergreen coniferous tree,
dense and columnar. Size:
at maturity up to 100ft
(30m).

CYDONIA *see*
    CHAENOMELES

CYPERUS
Sedge, Galingale, Umbrella
    plant, Papyrus, Paper
    reed
Cyperaceae
Perennial marginal
aquatic. Size: see var.

CYRTOMIUM
Japanese holly/Fishtail
  fern
Polypodiaceae
Evergreen tufted fern. Size:
up to 3 × 3ft (90 ×
90cm).

DAHLIA
Compositae
Tuberous perennial and
annual. All colours except
blue from mid summer.
Size: up to 5ft (1.5m).

DAVIDIA
Dove/Handkerchief tree
Nyssaceae (sometimes
classed in *Davidaceae*)
Deciduous tree. Creamy-
white bracts in late spring,
then autumn colour. Size:
at maturity 50ft (15m).
See var.

CYSTOPTERIS
Bladder fern
Polypodiaceae
Deciduous fern. Size:
small.

DANÄE
incl. Alexandrian laurel
Liliaceae
Evergreen bamboo-like
shrub. Greenish-yellow
fls., red bs. Size: 4 × 3ft
(1.2m × 90cm).

DECAISNEA
Lardizabalaceae
Deciduous erect shrub.
Yellowish-green fls.,
foliage and frs. Size: up to
15 × 8ft (4.5 × 2.5m).

CYTISUS
Broom, Florists' genista,
  Spanish gorse, Dyer's
  greenweed
Leguminosae
Deciduous or evergreen
shrub. Most colours except
blue from spring to late
summer. Size: up to 12 ×
12ft (3.5 × 3.5m). See
var.

DAPHNE
Thymelaeaceae
Deciduous, semi-evergreen
and evergreen shrub,
dwarf, mat-forming rock
plant. Purple/red/white/
yellow fls. in winter and
spring. Size: up to 6 × 5ft
(1.8 × 1.5m). See var.

DELPHINIUM
Larkspur
Ranunculaceae
Herbaceous perennial and
annual. Blue/pink/lilac/
cream fls. from early
summer. Size: up to 4½ ×
2ft (1.4m × 60cm).

DABOECIA
incl. St Dabeoc's/Irish
  heath
Ericaceae
Evergreen carpeting
shrub. Red/purple/pink/
white fls. from spring to
autumn. Size: up to 2 ×
2ft (60 × 60cm). See var.

DAVALLIA
incl. Squirrel's-foot/
  Hare's-foot fern
Polypodiaceae
Rhizomatous semi-
evergreen fern. Size: very
small.

DENDRANTHEMA
(previously
  CHRYSANTHEMUM)
Compositae
Perennial, evergreen sub-
shrubby rock plant and
annual. Red/pink/yellow/
white fls. in most seasons.
Size: up to 6 × 1½ft
(1.8m × 45cm). See var.

DENNSTAEDTIA
Hay-scented/Boulder fern
Polypodiaceae
Herbaceous perennial fern.
Size: 2 × 1½ft (60 × 45cm).

DESMODIUM
Leguminosae
Deciduous herbaceous
sub-shrub. Pink/lilac fls.
from late summer to
autumn. Size: 4 × 4ft
(1.2 × 1.2m).

DICENTRA
Bleeding heart,
   Dutchman's breeches
Fumariaceae
Herbaceous perennial and
evergreen rock plant.
Mauve/pink/white fls.
from mid spring. Size: up
to 1½ × 1ft (45 × 30cm).

DENTARIA
Toothwort
Cruciferae
Herbaceous perennial.
White/mauve fls. in
spring. Size: small.

DEUTZIA
Saxifragaceae (sometimes
classed in *Philadelphaceae*)
Deciduous, arching shrub.
White/pink fls. in spring
and early summer. Size: up
to 10 × 7ft (3 × 2m). See
var.

DICHELOSTEMMA
Brodiaea, Firecracker
   flower, Grass nut, Wild
   hyacinth, Blue-dicks
Amaryllidaceae
Corm. Lilac/white/yellow/
blue fls. Size: up to 2ft
(60cm).

DESCHAMPSIA
Tufted hair grass
Gramineae
Ornamental evergreen
grass. Size: 3 × 3ft (90 ×
90cm).

DIANTHUS
Carnation, Pink,
   Gilliflower, Sweet
   William
Caryophyllaceae
Evergreen perennial,
annual and rock plant.
Pink/red/purple/white/
yellow fls. in mid summer.
Size: up to 4 × 1ft
(1.2m × 30cm). See var.

DICTAMNUS
Rue, Dittany, Gas plant,
   Burning bush
Rutaceae
Herbaceous and evergreen
perennial and sub-shrub.
Size: up to 3 × 2ft (90 ×
60cm).

DESFONTAINEA
Loganiaceae (sometimes
classed in *Potaliaceae*)
Evergreen shrub. Scarlet-
yellow fls. in late summer.
Size: 8 × 5ft (2.5 ×
1.5m).

DIASCIA
Twinspur
Scrophulariaceae
Annual. Pink fls. in early
summer. Size: small.

DIERAMA
Wand flower, Angel's
   fishing rod
Iridaceae
Semi-evergreen corm.
Red/white fls. from mid
summer to autumn. Size:
up to 6 × 1½ft (1.8m ×
45cm).

DIERVILLA
Weigela, Bush
honeysuckle
Caprifoliaceae
Deciduous shrub. Pink/
white/yellow/red fls. in
late spring. Size: 7 × 6ft
(2 × 1.8m).

DIOSPYROS
Persimmon
Ebenaceae
Deciduous tree. Cream fls.
Foliage and frs. Size:
30 × 20ft (9 × 6m).

DORONICUM
Leopard's bane
Compositae
Perennial. Yellow fls. in
spring. Size: up to 3 × 1½ft
(90 × 45cm). See var.

DIETES
Iridaceae
Evergreen rhizomatous
perennial. Cream/white
fls. in spring or summer.
Size: up to 3 × 2ft (90 ×
60cm).

DIPELTA
Caprifoliaceae
Deciduous shrub. Pink/
creamy-white fls. Size:
10 × 6ft (3 × 1.8m).

DORYCNIUM
Canary clover
Leguminosae
Deciduous or semi-
evergreen low, spreading
shrub. White/pink/purple
fls. all summer. Size: 2 ×
2ft (60 × 60cm).

DIGITALIS
Foxglove
Scrophulariaceae
Perennial (evergreen) and
biennial. Cream-yellow/
pink/purple/red/white fls.
from early summer. Size:
up to 5 × 1½ft (1.5m ×
45cm).

DISANTHUS
Hamamelidaceae
Deciduous shrub. Autumn
colour. Size: 8 × 6ft
(2.5 × 1.8m).

DOUGLASIA
Primulaceae
Cushion-forming alpine.
Pink/yellow fls. in late
spring, early summer. Size:
very small.

DIMORPHOTHECA
Dwarf cape marigold,
African daisy
Compositae
Perennial sub-shrub,
evergreen rock plant and
annual. Rosy-purple/
cream/white/orange/
yellow fls. from late spring.
Size: 2 × 1ft (60 ×
30cm).

DISPORUM
Fairy bells/lantern
Liliaceae
Rhizomatous herbaceous
perennial. Creamy-white
fls. in spring, then bs. Size:
small.

DRACOCEPHALUM
Dragon's head
Labiatae
Perennial and annual.
Blue/yellow fls. in
summer. Size: up to 3 ×
2ft (90 × 60cm).

DRACUNCULUS
Dragon plant
Araceae
Tuberous perennial.
Green-maroon spathes.
Size: 3 × 1½ft (90 × 45cm).

DUCHESNIA
Ornamental strawberry
Rosaceae
Herbaceous (some semi-evergreen) trailing
perennial. Yellow fls. in early summer. Size: very small.

ECHINOPS
Globe thistle
Compositae
Perennial. Blue fls. in mid summer. Size: 5 × 2ft (1.5m × 60cm).

DREGEA
Wattakaka
Asclepiadaceae
Deciduous clinging woody climber. Creamy-white fls. in summer. Size: 10ft (3m).

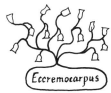

ECCREMOCARPUS
Chilean glory flower
Bignoniaceae
Evergreen perennial and annual climber. Scarlet/yellow fls. in summer and autumn. Size: 15ft (4.5m).

ECHIUM
Viper's bugloss
Boraginaceae
Annual. White/pink/red/purple/blue fls. in summer. Size: up to 3 × 1½ft (90 × 45cm).

DRYAS
Mountain avens
Rosaceae
Mat-forming sub-shrub. White/yellow fls. in early summer. Size: very small.

ECHINACEA
Purple coneflower
Compositae
Herbaceous perennial. White/purple/red/pink fls. in mid to late summer. Size: up to 4ft (1.2m).

EDGEWORTHIA
Paperbush
Thymelaeaceae
Evergreen shrub. Yellow fls. in late winter. Size: 6 × 5ft (1.8 × 1.5m).

DRYOPTERIS
Buckler/Wood/Shield fern
Polypodiaceae
Herbaceous perennial fern. Size: up to 4 × 3ft (1.2m × 90cm).

ECHINODORUS
incl. Amazon sword plant
Alismataceae
Herbaceous perennial shallow water marginal aquatic. Rosy-white fls. in summer. Size: ht. up to 2ft (60cm). See var.

EDRAIANTHUS
Grassy-bell
Campanulaceae
Herbaceous mat-forming rock plant. Blue/purple fls. in late spring. Size: very small.

EICHHORNIA
Water hyacinth
Pontederiaceae
Floating water plant.
Lavender-blue fls. in
summer. Size: ht. up to 2ft
(60cm), invasive.

EMILIA
Tassel flower, Paintbrush
Compositae
Annual. Red/yellow fls. all
summer. Size: small.

ERANTHUS
Winter aconite
Ranunculaceae
Tuberous clump-forming
perennial. Yellow fls. from
late winter to spring. Size:
very small.

ELAEAGNUS
Oleaster, Russian olive,
  Silverberry
Elaeagnaceae
Deciduous and evergreen
shrub. Bs. Size: up to 15 ×
15ft (4.5 × 4.5m).

ENKIANTHUS
Ericaceae
Deciduous shrub. Yellow/
white/red fls. in late
spring; autumn colour.
Size: up to 8 × 5ft (2.5 ×
1.5m).

EREMURUS
Foxtail lily, Desert candle
Liliaceae
Herbaceous perennial.
White/pink/yellow fls.
from early to mid summer.
Size: up to 10 × 3ft
(3m × 90cm). See var.

ELSHOLTZIA
Mint shrub
Labiatae
Herbaceous sub-shrub.
Purplish-pink fls. in late
summer and autumn. Size:
4 × 2ft (1.2m × 60cm).

EPILOBIUM
Willow herb, Evening
  primrose
Onagraceae
Herbaceous perennial and
rock plant. Red/pink/
white fls. in summer. Size:
up to $2\frac{1}{2}$ × $1\frac{1}{2}$ft (75 ×
45cm).

ERICA
Heaths, Heathers
Ericaceae
Evergreen erect and dwarf
shrub. White/pink/red/
mauve/purple fls. all
seasons. Size: up to 20ft
(6m). See var.

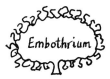

EMBOTHRIUM
Chilean fire bush
Proteaceae
Evergreen erect shrub.
Scarlet fls. in late spring.
Size: 40 × 13ft (12 ×
4m).

EPIMEDIUM
Barrenwort, Bishop's hat
Berberidaceae
Evergreen or semi-
evergreen perennial. Red/
yellow/pink fls. in early
spring; autumn colour.
Size: small.

ERIGERON
Fleabane
Compositae
Herbaceous perennial and
rock plant. Pink/violet/
blue/yellow fls. from late
spring to summer. Size:
small.

ERINUS
Fairy foxglove
Scrophulariaceae
Evergreen rock plant.
White/pink/red/purple fls.
from spring to mid
summer. Size: very small.

ERODIUM
Storksbill, Heron's-bill
Geraniaceae
Semi-evergreen rock plant.
Pink/yellow/white/lilac
fls. in early to mid
summer. Size: small.

ERYTHRONIUM
Dog's-tooth violet,
  Adder's-tongue,
  Avalanche/Fawn/Trout
  lily
Liliaceae
Bulb. White/yellow/pink/
purple fls. in spring. Size:
up to 2ft (60cm).

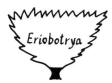

ERIOBOTRYA
Loquat, Japanese medlar
Rosaceae
Evergreen bushy tree.
White fls. in autumn, frs.
Size: 18 × 15ft (5.5 ×
4.5m).

ERYNGIUM
Umbelliferae
Herbaceous and evergreen
thistly perennial. Green/
blue/purple fls. in summer.
Size: 4 × 2ft (1.2m ×
60cm).

ESCALLONIA
Can be classed in
Escalloniaceae,
Saxifragaceae and
Crassulariaceae
Evergreen, semi-evergreen
or deciduous shrub, small
tree. White/pink/red fls.
from late summer to
autumn. Size: up to 10 ×
8ft (3 × 2.5m). See var.

ERIOPHORUM
Cotton grass
Cyperaceae
Rhizomatous marginal
aquatic. White fls. Size:
small.

ERYSIMUM
Dwarf wallflower, Treacle
  mustard, Prairie rocket
Cruciferae
Evergreen rock plant and
annual. Yellow/cream/
orange/violet fls. from
spring to summer. Size:
3 × 2ft (90 × 60cm). See
var.

ESCHSCHOLZIA
California poppy
Papaveraceae
Annual. Yellow/orange/
white/pink/red fls. all
summer. Size: small.

ERIOPHYLLUM
Compositae
Evergreen sub-shrub,
perennial and rock plant.
Yellow fls. in summer.
Size: small.

ERYTHRINA
Coral tree
Leguminosae
Deciduous and semi-
evergreen shrub and tree.
Red/orange-red fls. in
spring, summer and
autumn. Size: up to 20 ×
20ft (6 × 6m). See var.

EUCALYPTUS
Gum tree
Myrtaceae
Evergreen tree and shrub,
some weeping. Size: up to
100 × 30ft (30 × 9m).
See var.

EUCOMIS
Pineapple lily
Liliaceae
Bulb. White/greenish fls.
from mid to late summer.
Size: up to 5ft (1.5m).

EUPATORIUM
Joe Pye weed, White
snakeroot/sanicle,
Hemp agrimony
Compositae
Low-growing shrub and
erect perennial. Red/blue/
purple/white fls. in late
summer and autumn. Size:
up to 6 × 3ft (1.8m ×
90cm). See var.

FABIANA
Solanaceae
Evergreen shrub. White/
bluish-mauve fls. from late
spring to early summer.
Size: 7 × 7ft (2 × 2m).

EUCRYPHIA
Brush bush, Leatherwood
Eucryphiaceae
Deciduous or evergreen
shrub. Foliage and white
fls. from summer to
autumn. Size: up to 20 ×
10ft (6 × 3m). See var.

EUPHORBIA
incl. Spurge, Mole plant,
Snow-on-the-mountain,
Mexican fire plant
Euphorbiaceae
Evergreen sub-shrub,
herbaceous perennial,
annual. Yellow-green/red
fls. in spring and summer.
Size: up to 5 × 3ft
(1.5m × 90cm). See var.

FAGUS
Common beech
Fagaceae
Deciduous tree. Size: up to
100ft (30m). See var.

EUODIA
Ruticeae
Deciduous tree. White fls.
in late summer, red frs.
Size: 20 × 16ft (6 × 5m).

EURYOPS
Compositae
Evergreen shrub. Yellow
fls. in late spring. Size: 2 ×
4ft (60cm × 1.2m).

× FATSHEDERA
Araliaceae
Evergreen shrub, ground-
and wall-cover. Size: 6 ×
6ft (1.8 × 1.8m).

EUONYMUS
Spindle
Celastraceae
Deciduous and evergreen
tree, shrub and creeper.
Fls., frs. and autumn
colour. Size: up to 10 ×
10ft (3 × 3m). See var.

EXOCHORDA
Pearl bush
Rosaceae
Deciduous spreading
shrub. White fls. in late
spring. Size: up to 10 ×
10ft (3 × 3m). See var.

FATSIA
Castor oil plant
Araliaceae
Evergreen shrub. White
fls. in autumn. Size: 7 ×
7ft (2 × 2m).

FELICIA
Alpine aster, Blue/
  Kingfisher daisy
Compositae
Annual and evergreen
sub-shrub. Blue fls. in
summer. Size: small.

FILIPENDULA
incl. Meadowsweet,
  Dropwort, Queen of the
  prairie
Rosaceae
Perennial. White/pink fls.
in spring and summer.
Size: up to 8 × 2ft
(2.5m × 60cm). See var.

FRANKLINIA
Theaceae
Deciduous shrub or tree.
White fls. in late summer,
autumn colour. Size: 15 ×
10ft (4.5 × 3m).

FERULA
Giant fennel
Umbelliferae
Herbaceous perennial.
Yellow fls. in summer.
Size: up to 12ft (3.5m). See
var.

FORSYTHIA
incl. Golden ball
Oleaceae
Deciduous shrub, wall
climber, weeping, low
ground-cover. Yellow fls.
in early spring. Size: up to
10 × 8ft (3 × 2.5m). See
var.

FRAXINUS
Ash
Oleaceae
Deciduous tree, erect and
weeping. Some vars.
autumn colour. Size: up to
40 × 25ft (12 × 7.5m).
See var.

FESTUCA
Fescue
Gramineae
Evergreen perennial tuft-
forming ornamental grass.
Size: very small.

FOTHERGILLA
incl. Witch alder
Hamamelidaceae
Deciduous shrub. Creamy-
white fls. in spring,
autumn colour. Size: up to
10 × 7ft (3 × 2m). See
var.

FREESIA
Iridaceae
Herbaceous corm. White/
yellow/pink/orange/red/
purple fls. in winter and
spring. Size: small.

FICUS
Common fig
Moraceae
Deciduous shrubby fruit
tree. Frs. in autumn. Size:
up to 15 × 12ft (4.5 ×
3.5m). See var.

FRAGARIA
Ornamental strawberries
Rosaceae
Semi-evergreen perennial.
White/yellow fls. in early
summer then frs. Size: very
small.

FREMONTODENDRON/
  FREMONTIA
Flannel bush
Bombacaceae (sometimes
classed in *Sterculiaceae*)
Evergreen, semi-evergreen
upright or spreading
shrub. Yellow fls. from late
spring to mid autumn.
Size: up to 20 × 12ft (6 ×
3.5m).

FRITILLARIA
Fritillary, Guinea-hen flower, Adobe lily
Liliaceae
Bulb. Complex chequered fls. in spring. Size: up to 4ft (1.2m). See var.

GALAX
Diapensiaceae
Rhizomatous evergreen perennial. White fls. in early summer. Size: small.

GALTONIA
Summer hyacinth, Spire lily
Liliaceae
Bulb. White fls. in late summer. Size: 4 × 1ft (1.2m × 90cm).

FUCHSIA
Onagraceae
Deciduous or evergreen upright or trailing shrub or small tree. White/pink/purple/red fls. all summer. Size: up to 6 × 6ft (1.8 × 1.8m).

GALEGA
Goat's rue
Leguminosae
Herbaceous perennial. White/pink/mauve/violet-blue fls. in summer. Size: up to 5 × 3ft (1.5m × 90cm).

GARRYA
Silk tassel bush
Garryaceae
Evergreen shrub. Catkins in winter and spring. Size: 12 × 12ft (3.5 × 3.5m).

GAILLARDIA
Blanket flower
Compositae
Herbaceous perennial and annual. Yellow/brownish-red/red/orange fls. from summer to autumn. Size: up to 3 × 1½ft (90 × 45cm). See var.

GALEOBDOLON
Dead nettle, Yellow archangel
Labiatae
Semi-evergreen carpeting perennial. Yellow fls. in summer. Size: 2 × 2ft (60 × 60cm).

× GAULNETTYA
Ericaceae
Evergreen shrub. White/pink fls. from spring to early summer; red frs. Size: 3 × 3ft (90 × 90cm).

GALANTHUS
Snowdrop, Fair maids of February
Amaryllidaceae
White fls. from winter to early spring. Size: very small.

GALIUM
Sweet woodruff, Bedstraw
Rubiaceae
Herbaceous perennial ground cover. White fls. in early summer. Size: very small.

GAULTHERIA
incl. Wintergreen, Box berry, Canda tree, Checkerberry, Creeping tea berry, Partridge-berry
Ericaceae
Evergreen shrub. White/pink fls. in spring and summer. Bs. Size: up to 4 × 4ft (1.2 × 1.2m). See var.

GAURA
Onagraceae
Herbaceous perennial and annual. Pink/white fls. in summer and autumn. Size: 4 × 3ft (1.2m × 90cm).

GERANIUM
Cranesbill, Storksbill, Heron's-bill
Geraniaceae
Herbaceous, evergreen, semi-evergreen perennial and rock plant. Pink/red/blue/purple/white fls., spring to autumn. Size: up to 3 × 2½ft (90 × 75cm). See var.

GLADIOLUS
Sword/Corn lily
Iridaceae
Corm. Wide colour range (except blue) from early to late summer. Size: up to 4ft (1.2m). See var.

GELSEMIUM
Carolina/yellow jessamine
Loganiaceae
Evergreen twining climber. Yellow fls. from late spring to late summer. Size: up to 20ft (6m).

GEUM
Avens, Indian chocolate
Rosaceae
Herbaceous perennial and evergreen sub-shrubby mat-forming rock plant. Yellow/red/orange fls. in early summer. Size: up to 2 × 1½ft (60 × 45cm). See var.

GLAUCIDIUM
Ranunculaceae (sometimes classed in *Paeoniaceae* and in *Podophyllaceae*)
Herbaceous perennial. White/lilac fls. in late spring. Size: 2 × 2ft (60 × 60cm).

GENISTA
Broom, Gorse, Dyer's greenweed
Leguminosae
Deciduous shrub and tree, tall and dwarf vars. Yellow fls. in summer. Size: up to 15 × 15ft (4.5 × 4.5m).

GILLENIA
Bowman's root
Rosaceae
Perennial. White fls. in early summer. Size: 3 × 2ft (90 × 60cm).

GLAUCIUM
Horned/Sea poppy
Papaveraceae
Annual. Red/yellow/orange fls. in summer. Size: up to 2 × 1½ft (60 × 45cm).

GENTIANA
Gentian
Gentianaceae
Herbaceous evergreen and semi-evergreen perennial, alpine, biennial and annual. Blue/white/yellow fls. in spring, summer and autumn. Size: very small (except yellow var. 5 × 2ft (1.5m × 60cm).

GINKGO
Maidenhair tree
Ginkgoaceae
Deciduous coniferous tree. Frs. in early autumn. Size: at maturity 80ft (25m).

GLECHOMA
Ground ivy
Labiatae
Evergreen trailing and mat-forming perennial. Lavender fls. in late spring. Size: very small.

GLEDITSIA
Honey/Sweet locust
Leguminosae
Deciduous tree. Size: at maturity over 100ft (30m).

GREVILLEA
Spider flower, Silky oak, Firewheel
Proteaceae
Evergreen shrub or tree. Red/pink/cream/yellow/orange fls. from winter to summer. Size: up to 60 × 30ft (18 × 9m). See var.

GYMNOCLADUS
Kentucky coffee tree
Leguminosae
Deciduous foliage tree. Size: at maturity 50ft (15m).

GLOBULARIA
Globe daisy
Globulariaceae
Evergreen cushion-forming rock plant. Blue fls. in late spring. Size: very small.

GRISELINIA
Cornaceae
Evergreen shrub. Size: 15 × 10ft (4.5 × 3m).

GYPSOPHILA
Baby's breath, Chalk plant
Caryophyllaceae
Perennial, annual and trailing, mat-forming rock plant. White/pink fls. in summer. Size: up to 3 × 2ft (90 × 60cm).

GLYCERIA
Variegated manna-grass
Gramineae
Herbaceous perennial marginal aquatic. Size: up to 3ft (90cm).

GUNNERA
Gunneraceae (formerly in *Haloragaceae*)
Rhizomatous bog-liking herbaceous perennial. Size: up to 10 × 12ft (3 × 3.5m). See var.

HABERLEA
Gesneriaceae
Evergreen rock plant. Mauve/white fls. in early summer. Size: very small.

GOMPHRENA
Globe amaranth
Amaranthaceae
Annual, biennial, perennial. Purple/red/pink/white/yellow fls. in summer. Size: small.

GYMNOCARPIUM
Oak fern
Polypodiaceae
Rhizomatous fern. Size: small.

HABRANTHUS
incl. Zephyr lily, Rain lily, Flowers of the west wind
Amaryllidaceae
Bulb. Pink/red/yellow fls. in summer and autumn. Size: small.

HACQUETIA
Dondia
Umbelliferae
Rhizomatous perennial creeping rock plant. Yellow fls. in early spring. Size: very small.

HAKEA
incl. Pincushion tree, Sea-urchin tree
Proteaceae
Evergreen shrub and pine-like tree. White/crimson fls. in early summer or late autumn. Size: up to 30 × 20ft (9 × 6m). See var.

HALESIA
incl. Mountain snowball tree, Carolina/Mountain silverbell tree, Snowdrop tree
Styraceae
Deciduous large shrub or small tree. White/pink fls. in late spring. Size: up to 40 × 30ft (12 × 9m). See var.

× HALIMIOCISTUS
Cistaceae
Evergreen shrub, bushy and prostrate. White blotched fls. in spring and summer. Size: up to 2 × 4ft (60cm × 1.2m).

HALIMIUM
Cistaceae
Evergreen shrub. White/yellow blotched fls. from late spring to mid summer. Size: up to 3 × 4ft (90cm × 1.2m).

HAMAMELIS
Witch hazel
Hamamelidaceae
Deciduous shrub or small tree. Yellow/red fls. in late winter, early spring. Some vars. autumn colour. Size: 8 × 8ft (2.5 × 2.5m).

HEBE
Veronica
Scrophulariaceae
Evergreen shrub and dwarf hummock-forming rock plant. Purple/lilac/white/pink fls. from spring to winter. Size: up to 10 × 10ft (3 × 3m). See var.

HEDERA
Ivy
Araliaceae
Evergreen shrub, woody climber and ground-cover. Leaf colour. Size: up to 50ft (15m). See var.

HEDYOTIS
Rubiaceae
Evergreen perennial prostrate rock plant. White/blue fls. in late spring to summer. Size: very small.

HEDYSARUM
incl. Mongolian sweet vetch, French honeysuckle
Leguminosae
Deciduous shrub, sub-shrub, perennial and biennial. Rosy-purple fls. all summer. Size: up to 5 × 7ft (1.5 × 2m).

HELENIUM
Sneezeweed
Compositae
Herbaceous perennial. Yellow/red/orange fls. in mid to late summer. Size: up to 5 × 1½ft (1.5m × 45cm).

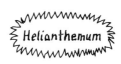

HELIANTHEMUM
Rock/Sun rose
Cistaceae
Evergreen semi-prostrate spreading sub-shrub. Yellow/reds/orange/white fls. from spring to autumn. Size: small.

HELIANTHUS
Sunflower
Compositae
Annual and perennial.
Yellow fls. from mid to late
summer. Size: up to 10ft
(3m).

HELIOTROPIUM
Cherry pie, Heliotrope
Boraginaceae
Annual or perennial.
Purple/blue/white fls. in
summer. Size: 2 × 1½ft
(60 × 45cm).

HEMEROCALLIS
Day lily
Liliaceae
Herbaceous and semi-
evergreen perennial, some
rhizomatous. Cream/
yellow/orange/red/lilac/
purple fls. from summer to
autumn. Size: up to 3 ×
2ft (90 × 60cm). See var.

HELICHRYSUM
incl. Everlastings, Curry
plant, Immortelles,
Strawflower
Compositae
Evergreen shrub and
deciduous perennial, rock
plant, annual. White/
cream/yellow fls. in
summer. Size: up to 8 ×
6ft (2.5 × 1.8m). See var.

HELIPTERUM
incl. Sunray, Everlastings,
Immortelles
Compositae
Annual. Red/pink/white
fls. in summer. Size: small.

HEPATICA
Ranunculaceae
Semi-evergreen perennial
rock plant. Mauve/purple/
blue/white/pink/red fls. in
early spring. Size: very
small.

HELICTOTRICHON
Gramineae
Blue oat grass
Evergreen perennial
ornamental grass. Size:
4 × 3ft (1.2m × 90cm).

HELLEBORUS
Christmas/Lenten rose
Ranunculaceae
Evergreen herbaceous
perennial. Subtle mixed
colours from winter to
early spring. Size: up to
2 × 2ft (60 × 60cm). See
var.

HERMODACTYLUS
Snake's-head iris
Iridaceae
Tuberous perennial. Olive-
green fls. in mid to late
spring. Size: small.

HELIOPSIS
Compositae
Herbaceous perennial.
Yellow fls. all summer.
Size: 4 × 2ft (1.2m ×
60cm).

HELONIAS
Swamp pink
Liliaceae
Rhizomatous perennial
bog plant. Pink-purple fls.
in spring. Size: 3 × 2ft
(90 × 60cm).

HESPERIS
incl. Sweet/Dame's rocket,
Dame's or damask violet
Cruciferae
Evergreen perennial and
annual. White/pale purple
fls. in early summer. Size:
3 × 2ft (90 × 60cm).

HETEROMELES
incl. Toyon, Christmas berry
Rosaceae
Evergreen spreading shrub or tree. White fls. late summer, red frs. Size: 12 × 10ft (3.5 × 3m).

HIERACIUM
Hawkweed
Compositae
Deciduous and evergreen perennial. Yellow fls. in summer, silvery-grey lvs. Size: small.

HOLODISCUS
incl. Cream bush, Ocean spray
Rosaceae
Deciduous spreading shrub. Creamy fls. in summer. Size: 12 × 12ft (3.5 × 3.5m).

HEUCHERA
Saxifragaceae
Semi-evergreen perennial. Cream/white/pink/greenish-yellow/red fls. in late spring and summer. Size: up to 3 × 1ft (90 × 30cm).

HIPPOPHAË
incl. Sea buckthorn, Sallow thorn
Elaeagnaceae
Deciduous foliage shrub. Size: up to 15 × 15ft (4.5 × 4.5m).

HORDEUM
Squirrel-tail grass
Gramineae
Ornamental annual grass. Size: 2½ × 1ft (75 × 30cm).

× HEUCHERELLA
Saxifragaceae
Hybrid perennial. Pink fls. in spring and summer. Size: small.

HOHERIA
Lacebark
Malvaceae
Deciduous, evergreen and semi-evergreen tree and shrub. White fls. in mid summer. Size: up to 30ft (9m) or more. See var.

HOSTA
incl. Plantain lily, Funkia
Liliaceae or *Funkiaceae*
Deciduous perennial. Decorative lvs., white/purple fls. in summer. Size: up to 3 × 2½ft (90 × 75cm). See var.

HIBISCUS
incl. Tree hollyhock, Flower of an hour, Rose of Sharon, Rose mallow
Malvaceae
Deciduous and evergreen tree, shrub, perennial and annual. Wide colour range, summer to autumn. Size: up to 10 × 6ft (3 × 1.8m). See var.

HOLCUS
Variegated creeping soft grass
Gramineae
Perennial ornamental grass. Size: small.

HOTTONIA
Water violet
Primulaceae
Deciduous perennial submerged water plant. Pink/lilac/whitish fls. in summer. Size: indefinite spread.

HOUTTUYNIA
Saururaceae
Rhizomatous herbaceous perennial marginal aquatic. Coloured lvs., white fls. in summer. Size: very small height but invasive spreader.

HYACINTHUS
Hyacinth
Liliaceae
Bulb. White/blue/pink/red/yellow/orange fls. in spring. Size: small.

HYPERICUM
incl. St John's wort, Rose of Sharon
Guttiferae (sometimes classed in *Hypericaceae*)
Evergreen or semi-evergreen shrub, perennial and deciduous rock plant. Yellow fls. in summer and autumn. Size: up to 7 × 7ft (2 × 2m). See var.

HOVENIA
Japanese raisin tree
Rhamnaceae
Deciduous tree. Foliage. Size: 20 × 15ft (6 × 4.5m).

HYDRANGEA
Saxifragaceae (sometimes classed in *Hydrangeaceae*)
Deciduous or evergreen shrub and self-clinging climber. White/pink/blue/red fls. in summer and autumn. Size: up to 15 × 10ft (4.5 × 3m). See var.

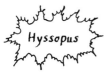

HYSSOPUS
Hyssop
Labiatae
Herbaceous perennial sub-shrub. White/pink/purple-blue fls. from mid to late summer. Size: small.

HUMULUS
Hop, Bittersweet
Cannabinaceae
Herbaceous perennial and annual twining climber. Leaf colour. Size: up to 20ft (6m).

HYDROCHARIS
incl. Frogbit, Water soldier
Hydrocharitaceae
Deciduous perennial floating water plant. White fls. in summer. Size: ht. very small, spr. up to 3ft (1m).

IBERIS
Candytuft
Cruciferae
Evergreen and semi-evergreen bushy sub-shrub, perennial and annual. White/pink/purple/red/lavender-blue fls. in spring and early summer. Size: very small.

HUNNEMANNIA
incl. Mexican tulip poppy, Golden cup
Papaveraceae
Perennial or annual. Yellow fls. all summer. Size: up to 3ft (90cm).

HYLOMECON
Papaveraceae
Herbaceous perennial. Yellow fls. in spring. Size: small.

IDESIA
Flacourtiaceae
Deciduous tree. Yellow fls. in summer, then red bs. Size: 20 × 15ft (6 × 4.5m).

ILEX
Holly, Winterberry,
  Inkberry
Aquifoliaceae
Evergreen or deciduous
tree and shrub, some
dwarf or prostrate vars.
Coloured bs. in autumn.
Size: up to 70ft (20m). See
var.

INULA
Compositae
Perennial, some
rhizomatous. Yellow/
orange fls. all summer.
Size: up to 6 × 3ft
(1.8m × 90cm). See var.

IRIS
Iridaceae
Rhizomatous or bulbous
evergreen and deciduous
herbaceous perennial,
dwarf vars. for rock
gardens and marginal
aquatic plants. Most
colours in spring and early
summer. Size: from small
to 4ft (1.2m) high. See var.

IMPATIENS
Balsam, Touch-me-not,
  Jewel weed, Busy Lizzie,
  Patient Lucy
Balsaminaceae
Annual. Most colours
(except blue) during long
summer season. Size: up to
5 × 2ft (1.5m × 60cm).
See var.

IONOPSIDIUM
Violet cress, Diamond
  flower
Cruciferae
Annual. Mauve/white fls.
all summer. Size: very
small.

ISATIS
Dyer's woad
Cruciferae
Perennial and biennial.
Yellow fls. early summer.
Size: 3 × 1½ft (90 ×
45cm).

INCARVILLEA
Bignoniaceae
Herbaceous perennial.
Pink fls. in early summer.
Size: 2 × 1ft (60 ×
30cm).

IPHEION
Spring star-flower
Amaryllidaceae (sometimes
classed in *Liliaceae*)
Bulb. Blue/white/yellow
fls. in spring. Size: very
small.

ITEA
Sweet spire
Saxifragaceae (sometimes
classed in *Escalloniaceae*)
Deciduous or evergreen
shrub. Greenish/creamy-
white fls. in mid and late
summer; autumn colour.
Size: up to 10 × 10ft (3 ×
3m). See var.

INDIGOFERA
Indigo bush
Leguminosae
Deciduous shrub. Pink-
purplish fls. from summer
to autumn. Size: up to 6 ×
6ft (1.8 × 1.8m).

IPOMOEA
incl. Morning glory, Blue
  dawn flower,
  Moonflower, Moonvine,
  Cardinal climber,
  Cypress vine
Convolvulaceae
Tuberous perennial,
climber and annual. Many
colours in summer. Size: to
10ft (3m). See var.

IXIA
African corn lily
Iridaceae
Herbaceous corm. Many
colours (except blue) fls. in
spring to early summer.
Size: small.

JASMINUM
Jasmine, Jessamine
Oleaceae
Evergreen, semi-evergreen and deciduous shrub, perennial climber and dwarf trailing rock plant. Yellow/white/pink/red fls. from mid winter to late summer. Size: up to 30ft (9m). See var.

JUNCUS
Corkscrew rush
Juncaceae
Herbaceous perennial marginal aquatic. Foliage. Size: small.

KALOPANAX
Araliaceae
Deciduous tree. White fls. in autumn. Size: 25 × 20ft (7.5 × 6m).

JEFFERSONIA
Berberidaceae (sometimes classed in *Podophyllaceae*)
Herbaceous perennial, low-growing for ground-cover. White/blue fls. in late spring. Size: small.

JUNIPERUS
Juniper
Cupressaceae
Evergreen coniferous tree and shrub: columnar, pyramidal, drooping, bushy and prostrate. Size: varies greatly, up to 40ft (12m). See var.

KERRIA
incl. Jew's mallow, Bachelor's/Sailor's buttons
Rosaceae
Deciduous arching shrub. Yellow fls. in late spring. Size: up to 10ft (3m). See var.

JOVIBARBA
Houseleek
Crassulaceae
Evergreen succulent rock plant. Yellow fls. in mid summer. Size: very small.

KALMIA
incl. American/Mountain laurel, Calico bush, Spoon wood, Lambkill
Ericaceae
Evergreen shrubs and dwarf alpine. White/pink/red fls. in early spring. Size: up to 10 × 8ft (3 × 2.5m). See var.

KIRENGESHOMA
Saxifragaceae (sometimes classed in *Hydrangeaceae*)
Perennial. Yellow fls. in late summer. Size: up to $3\frac{1}{2}$ × 3ft (1.1m × 60cm).

JUGLANS
Walnut, Butternut
Juglandaceae
Deciduous tree. Catkins, edible nuts. Size: up to 70ft (20m). See var.

KALMIOPSIS
Ericaceae
Evergreen dwarf shrub. Rosy-purple fls. in spring. Size: small.

KNAUTIA
Dipsacaceae
Perennial and annual. Crimson/blue-lilac fls. in summer. Size: 2 × 2ft (60 × 60cm).

KNIPHOFIA
incl. Red-hot poker, Torch
 lily
Liliaceae
Deciduous and evergreen
perennial. Cream/yellow/
red/orange fls. from early
summer to autumn. Size:
up to 5ft (1.5m). See var.

KOCHIA
incl. Burning bush,
 Summer cypress
Chenopodiaceae
Annual bush for foliage.
Size: 3 × 2ft (90 ×
60cm).

KOELERIA
Gramineae
Evergreen perennial
ornamental grass. Size:
2 × 1ft (60 × 30cm).

KOELREUTERIA
incl. Soapberry, Golden
 rain tree, Pride of India,
 Varnish tree
Sapindaceae
Deciduous tree and shrub.
Yellow fls. in summer,
then frs. Size: to 40ft
(12m) or more.

KOLKWITZIA
Beauty bush
Caprifoliaceae
Deciduous shrub. White/
pink fls. in late spring. Size:
up to 10 × 8ft (3 ×
2.5m).

× LABURNOCYTISUS
Leguminosae
Botanically curious
deciduous tree. Copper-
pink fls. from late spring.
Size: up to 20 × 15ft (6 ×
4.5m).

LABURNUM
Golden chain/rain
Leguminosae
Deciduous small tree.
Yellow fls. in late spring.
Size: up to 20 × 15ft (6 ×
4.5m). See var.

LACTUCA
incl. Mountain sow thistle
Compositae
Thistly perennial. Bluish
fls. in summer. Size: up to
6 × 2ft (1.8m × 60cm).

LAGERSTROEMIA
Crape myrtle
Lythraceae
Evergreen and deciduous
tree and shrub. Red/pink/
purple/white fls. in
summer; autumn colour.
Size: up to 20 × 10ft (6 ×
3m).

LAGURUS
incl. Hare's-tail, Rabbit's-
 tail grass
Gramineae
Ornamental annual wild
grass. Size: small.

LAMIUM/LAMIASTRATUM
incl. Dead nettle, Yellow
 archangel
Labiatae
Evergreen and herbaceous
perennial ground-cover.
Pink/red/purple/white fls.
in spring and summer.
Size: small.

LARDIZABALA
Akebia
Lardizabalaceae
Evergreen and semi-
evergreen twining
perennial climber. Purple/
white fls. in winter and
spring. Size: up to 40ft
(12m). See var.

LARIX
Larch, Tamarack
Pinaceae
Deciduous conical or weeping tree. Size: up to 100ft (30m).

LAVATERA
Tree mallow
Malvaceae
Evergreen and semi-evergreen shrub, sub-shrub, annual and biennial. Pink/purple/white fls. from early summer to autumn. Size: up to 7 × 5ft (2 × 1.5m). See var.

LEONOTIS
Lion's ear, Lion's tail
Labiatae
Evergreen shrub. Orange-red fls. in autumn. Size: 6 × 5ft (1.8 × 1.5m).

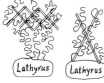

LATHYRUS
Sweet pea, Vetchling
Leguminosae
Herbaceous perennial, annual and climber. Most colours in summer and autumn. Size: up to 10ft (3m). See var.

LAYIA
Tidy tips
Compositae
Bushy annual. Yellow fls. in summer and autumn. Size: small.

LEONTOPODIUM
Edelweiss
Compositae
Evergreen perennial rock plant. White fls. in late spring. Size: very small.

LAURUS
Sweet bay, Bay laurel
Lauraceae
Evergreen shrub and small tree. Size: up to 12 × 6ft (3.5 × 1.8m). See var.

LEDUM
incl. Labrador tea, Wild rosemary
Ericaceae
Evergreen low-growing shrub. White fls. in late spring. Size: up to 3 × 3ft (90 × 90cm).

LEPTOSPERMUM
incl. Tea tree, Manuka
Myrtaceae
Evergreen shrub or small tree. White/pink fls. in early summer. Size: up to 20 × 15ft (6 × 4.5m). See var.

LAVANDULA
Lavender
Labiatae
Evergreen shrub. Pink/purple/white fls. in summer. Size: up to 3 × 4ft (90cm × 1.2m). See var.

LEIOPHYLLUM
Ericaceae
Evergreen dwarf shrub. White fls. in late spring. Size: small.

LESPEDEZA
Bush clover
Leguminosae
Herbaceous deciduous sub-shrub. Rosy-purple fls. in late summer. Size: up to 8 × 10ft (2.5 × 3m).

LEUCOCORYNE
incl. Ipheion, Star-flower
Amaryllidaceae
Bulb. White/violet-blue fls.
in spring. Size: very small.

LEYCESTERIA
Flowering nutmeg,
    Himalayan honeysuckle
Caprifoliaceae
Deciduous shrub. White
fls. in mid summer, then
purplish frs. Size: up to
8 × 6ft (2.5 × 1.8m).

LIGULARIA
incl. Golden ray, Leopard
    plant
Compositae
Perennial. Orange/yellow
fls. in mid summer. Size:
up to 6 × 3ft (1.8m ×
90cm).

LEUCOJUM
Snowflake, Loddon lily
Amaryllidaceae
Greenish-white fls. in
various seasons. Size: up to
2ft (60cm). See var.

LIATRIS
Gay feather, Blazing star
Compositae
Tuberous thistly
perennial. White/pink/
mauve/purple fls. in
summer. Size: up to 6 ×
1½ft (1.8m × 45cm). See
var.

LIGUSTRUM
Privet
Oleaceae
Evergreen, semi-evergreen
and deciduous tree and
shrub. White fls. in
summer. Size: up to 25 ×
20ft (7.5 × 6m). See var.

LEUCOTHOË
Ericaceae
Evergreen and semi-
evergreen shrub. White fls.
in summer; autumn
colour. Size: up to 6 × 4ft
(1.8 × 1.2m). See var.

LIBERTIA
Iridaceae
Rhizomatous herbaceous
perennial. White/green fls.
in late spring and summer.
Size: up to 3ft (90cm).

LILIUM
Lily
Liliaceae
Bulb. Most colours except
blue in summer. Size: up to
8ft (2.5m). See var.

LEWISIA
Bitter root
Portulacaceae
Herbaceous and evergreen
alpine. White/pink/
orange/red fls. in spring
and early summer. Size:
very small.

LIBOCEDRUS *see*
    CALOCEDRUS

LIMNANTHES
Poached-egg flower
Limnanthaceae
Annual. White fls. from
late spring to mid summer.
Size: very small.

LIMONIUM
Sea-lavender, Statice
Plumbaginaceae
Evergreen perennial,
biennial and annual. Fls.
in wide range of colours in
late summer. Size: up to
2 × 3ft (60 × 90cm). See
var.

LINARIA
Toadflax, Bunny rabbits
Scrophulariaceae
Perennial, evergreen
trailing rock plant and
annual. Yellow/purple/
pink fls. in spring, summer
and autumn. Size: up to
4 × 2ft (1.2m × 60cm).
See var.

LINDERA
Spice bush, Spicewood,
   Benjamin bush
Lauraceae
Deciduous and evergreen
shrub and tree. Yellow fls.;
frs. and autumn colour.
Size: up to 10 × 6ft (3 ×
1.8m). See var.

LINNAEA
Twin flower
Caprifoliaceae
Evergreen creeping sub-
shrubby perennial. Pink
fls. in early summer. Size:
very small.

LINUM
Flax
Linaceae
Herbaceous perennial,
shrubby rock plant and
annual. Blue/pink/red/
yellow/white fls. from
early to mid summer. Size:
up to 2 × 1ft (60 ×
30cm).

LIPPIA *see* ALOYSIA

LIQUIDAMBAR
Sweet gum
Hamamelidaceae
Deciduous columnar or
pyramidal tree or large
bush. Foliage and autumn
colour. Size: up to 80 ×
40ft (25 × 12m). See var.

LIRIODENDRON
Tulip tree
Magnoliaceae
Deciduous tree. Greenish-
yellow fls. in early
summer. Size: at maturity
up to 100ft (30m).

LIRIOPE
Lily-turf
Liliaceae
Evergreen rhizomatous
perennial ground-cover.
White/pinkish-purple fls.
from mid summer to
autumn. Size: small.

LITHODORA
Lithospermum
Boraginaceae
Evergreen carpeting sub-
shrub. Blue fls. all
summer. Size: very small.

LOBELIA
Cardinal flower
Lobeliaceae (sometimes
classed in *Campanulaceae*)
Herbaceous perennial and
trailing annual. Red/
purple/white/blue fls. all
summer. Size: up to 4 ×
1ft (1.2m × 30cm). See
var.

LOBULARIA
Sweet alyssum
Cruciferae
Annual. White/lilac/
purple fls. in summer. Size:
very small.

LOMATIA
Proteaceae
Evergreen shrub and small tree. Red/white/yellow fls. in summer. Size: up to 30 × 15ft (9 × 4.5m). See var.

LUNARIA
Honesty, Money plant, Moonwort, Satin flower
Cruciferae
Herbaceous perennial and biennial. Purple/lilac/white fls. in summer. Size: up to 3½ × 2ft (1.1m × 60cm). See var.

LYSICHITON
Skunk cabbage, Bog arum
Araceae
Rhizomatous perennial marginal aquatic and bog plant. Yellow and white spathes in spring. Size: 4 × 2ft (1.2m × 60cm).

LONICERA
Honeysuckle, Twinberry, Chinese woodbine
Caprifoliaceae
Evergreen, semi-evergreen and deciduous shrub and climber. Pink/yellow/white/red fls. from late winter. Size: up to 80ft (25m). See var.

LUPINUS
Tree lupin, Lupin
Leguminosae
Deciduous semi-woody shrub, herbaceous perennial and annual. Wide range of colours in summer. Size: up to 8 × 8ft (2.5 × 2.5m). See var.

LYSIMACHIA
Loosestrife, Moneywort, Creeping Jenny
Primulaceae
Herbaceous and evergreen perennial. Yellow/white fls. in summer. Size: up to 4 × 2ft (1.2m × 60cm). See var.

LOQUAT *see* **ERIOBOTRYA**

LYCHNIS
incl. Campion, Catchflies, Flower of Jove, Jerusalem/Maltese cross, Rose of heaven
Caryophyllaceae
Perennial, rock plant, biennial and annual. Red/orange/pink/white fls. in spring and summer. Size: up to 3ft (90cm). See var.

LYTHRUM
Purple loosestrife
Lythraceae
Herbaceous perennial. Red/purple/pink fls. all summer. Size: up to 5 × 1½ft (1.5m × 45cm). See var.

LOTUS
Winged pea
Leguminosae
Semi-evergreen perennial and evergreen trailing sub-shrub. Red fls. in summer. Size: 2 × 3ft (60 × 90cm).

LYCORIS
incl. Spider lily, Resurrection lily, Autumn amaryllis
Amaryllidaceae
Perennial bulb. Yellow/red/pink/lilac fls. in late summer. Size: small.

MACLEAYA
Plume poppy
Papaveraceae
Herbaceous perennial. Creamy-white/pink fls. in summer. Size: up to 7 × 3ft (2m × 90cm).

MAGNOLIA
incl. Cucumber tree, Pink
tulip tree, Yulan, Lily
tree
Magnoliaceae
Evergreen and deciduous
tree and shrub. White/
cream/pink/crimson/
purple fls. from late winter
to summer. Size: up to 90ft
(25m). See var.

× MAHOBERBERIS
Berberidaceae
Evergreen shrub. Foliage
and yellow fls. in late
spring. Size: 6 × 4ft
(1.8 × 1.2m).

MAHONIA
Oregon grape, Leatherleaf
mahonia
Berberidaceae
Evergreen shrub. Yellow
fls. in winter. Size: up to
10 × 12ft (3 × 3.5m).
See var.

MALCOLMIA
Virginia stock
Cruciferae
Annual. Red/lilac/rose/
white fls. from spring. Size:
very small.

MALOPE
Mallow-wort
Malvaceae
Annual. Purple-rose fls. all
summer. Size: 3 × 1ft
(90 × 30cm).

MALUS
Apple, Crabapple
Rosaceae
Deciduous fruiting tree
and shrub. Pink/white/
red/yellow fls. in spring.
Colourful frs. and some
vars. autumn colour. Size:
up to 20 × 20ft (6 × 6m).
See var.

MALVA
True mallow
Malvaceae
Herbaceous perennial.
Pink/lavender fls. in early
summer to late autumn.
Size: up to 4 × 2ft
(1.2m × 60cm).

MALVASTRUM *see*
ANISODONTEA

MARRUBIUM
Horehound
Labiatae
Herbaceous perennial.
White fls. in summer, grey
woolly foliage. Size: small.

MATRICARIA
incl. Feverfew
Compositae
Perennial and annual.
Yellow/white fls. in
summer. Size: small.

MATTEUCCIA
Ostrich fern, Shuttlecock
fern
Polypodiaceae
Herbaceous perennial fern.
Size: up to 6ft (1.8m). See
var.

MATTHIOLA
Stock, Gilliflower
Cruciferae
Annual and biennial. Most
colours (except blue and
orange) in summer. Size:
small.

MAZUS
Scrophulariaceae
Perennial mat-forming rock plant. White/violet/purple-blue fls. in summer. Size: very small.

MELISSA
Lemon/Common balm
Labiatae
Some vars. gold lvs. Size: $2 \times 1\frac{1}{2}$ft (60×45cm).

MENYANTHES
Bog/Buck bean, Marsh trefoil
Menyanthaceae (sometimes classed in *Gentianaceae*)
Rhizomatous herbaceous perennial marginal aquatic. Pinkish-white fls. in spring and summer. Size: small.

MECONOPSIS
incl. Himalayan blue/Welsh/Harebell poppy
Papaveraceae
Herbaceous perennial. Blue/purple/yellow/white/red fls. in spring or summer. Size: up to 5×2ft (1.5m $\times 60$cm). See var.

MELITTIS
Bastard balm
Labiatae
Herbaceous perennial. White-pink striped fls. from late spring to mid summer. Size: small.

MENZIESIA
Ericaceae
Deciduous shrub. Purplish-pink/cream/yellowish-green fls. in late spring. Size: up to 5×3ft (1.5m $\times 90$cm). See var.

MELIA
incl. Toon, Chinese cedar, Bead tree, China-berry, Texas umbrella tree
Meliaceae
Deciduous tree. White/lilac fls. in spring. Size: up to 30×30ft (9×9m). See var.

MENTHA
Mint
Labiatae
Culinary herb, herbaceous perennial, rock plant and marginal aquatic. Pinkish-purple fls. in summer. Size: up to 3×2ft (90×60cm). See var.

MERTENSIA
Virginia bluebell/cowslip
Boraginaceae
Perennial and ground-cover. Blue/pink fls. in spring. Size: up to 3×2ft (90×60cm). See var.

MELIANTHUS
Honey flower
Melianthaceae
Herbaceous sprawling sub-shrub. Foliage. Size: up to 8×10ft (2.5×3m).

MENTZELIA
Blazing star
Loasaceae
Bushy annual. Yellow fls. in mid summer. Size: small.

MESEMBRYANTHEMUM
Ice plant, Sea fig, Livingstone daisy
Aizoaceae
Low, spreading annual. Red/pink/orange/yellow/white fls. all summer. Size: very small.

MESPILUS
Medlar
Rosaceae
Deciduous fruit tree.
White/tinged pink fls. in
early summer. Size: 15 ×
18ft (4.5 × 5.5m).

MIMULUS
Monkey flower, Musk
Scrophulariaceae
Perennial, semi-evergreen
sub-shrub and dwarf mat-
forming rock plant. Most
colours, multi-coloured
and blotched fls. in
summer. Size: up to 4 ×
2ft (1.2m × 60cm). See
var.

MOLINIA
Indian/Moor grass
Gramineae
Herbaceous, perennial
ornamental grass in
autumn and winter. Size:
2 × 2ft (60 × 60cm).

METASEQUOIA
Dawn redwood
Taxodiaceae
Deciduous coniferous tree.
Autumn colour. Size: up to
60 × 16ft (18 × 5m).

MIRABILIS
Four-o'clock plant, Marvel
of Peru
Nyctaginaceae
Annual. Pink/white/red/
yellow and mixed coloured
fls. all summer. Size: up to
3 × 1ft (90 × 30cm).

MOLTKIA
Boraginaceae
Evergreen, semi-evergreen
and deciduous sub-shrub
and perennial, ground-
cover. Blue fls. in early
summer. Size: small.

MILIUM
Bowles' golden grass
Gramineae
Herbaceous perennial
ornamental grass. Size: up
to 2 × 1ft (60 × 30cm).

MISCANTHUS
Silver grass, Eulalia
Gramineae
Herbaceous perennial
ornamental grass. Size: up
to 10 × 3ft (3m × 90cm).
See var.

MOLUCCELLA
Bells of Ireland, Shell
flower, Molucca balm
Labiatae
Perennial and annual.
White/green fls. in
summer. Size: up to 2ft
(60cm).

MILLA
Ipheion, Spring-star flower
Amaryllidaceae (sometimes
classed in *Liliaceae*)
Bulb. White/violet-blue fls.
in spring and summer.
Size: very small.

MITCHELLA
Partridge berry
Rubiaceae
Evergreen trailing, mat-
forming rock plant.
Pinkish-white fls. in
summer, red bs. Size: very
small.

MONARDA
Sweet bergamot, Oswego
tea, Bee balm
Labiatae
Herbaceous perennial.
Red/pink/purple/white fls.
all summer. Size: 3 × 1½ft
(90 × 45cm).

MORAEA
Butterfly/African/Peacock iris, Natal lily
Iridaceae
Corm. White/yellow/blue fls. in winter or summer. Size: up to 3ft (90cm). See var.

MORINA
Whorl flower
Dipsacaceae
Evergreen thistly perennial. White ageing through pink to crimson fls. in mid summer. Size: 3 × 1½ft (90 × 45cm).

MORISIA
Cruciferae
Evergreen perennial rock plant. Yellow fls. all spring. Size: small.

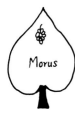

MORUS
Mulberry
Moraceae
Deciduous fruit tree. Edible frs. Size: up to 40 × 50ft (12 × 15m). See var.

MUEHLENBECKIA
Wire-vine, Maidenhair vine
Polygonaceae
Deciduous or evergreen twining climber or prostrate vars. White fls. mid summer then white frs. Size: up to 6ft (1.8m).

MUTISIA
Climbing gazania
Compositae
Evergreen perennial climber. Yellow/orange/pink fls. from summer to autumn. Size: up to 10ft (3m). See var.

MYOSOTIDIUM
Giant/Chatham Island forget-me-not
Boraginaceae
Evergreen perennial ground-cover. Blue fls. in spring. Size: small.

MYOSOTIS
Forget-me-not
Boraginaceae
Perennial, biennial, annual, and evergreen marginal aquatic. Blue/pink fls. in spring and summer. Size: small.

MYRICA
Bayberry, Sweet gale, Bog or Wax myrtle
Myricaceae
Deciduous, semi-evergreen and evergreen shrub. Catkins then frs. Size: up to 12 × 8ft (3.5 × 2.5m). See var.

MYRTUS
Myrtle
Myrtaceae
Evergreen tree and shrub. White fls. in summer. Size: shrub up to 20 × 15ft (6 × 4.5m), tree up to 40ft (12m). See var.

NANDINA
Chinese sacred/heavenly bamboo
Berberidaceae (sometimes classed in *Nandinaceae*)
Evergreen shrub. White fls. in mid summer then frs. Size: up to 6 × 3ft (1.8m × 90cm). See var.

NARCISSUS
Daffodil, Narcissus, Jonquil
Amaryllidaceae
Bulb, mainly spring-flowering. Yellow/white/cream/orange fls. Size: small.

NEMESIA
Scrophulariaceae
Annual. White/yellow/
orange/red/purple/blue
fls. in summer. Size: small.

NERIUM
incl. Oleander, Rose-bay
Apocynaceae
Evergreen shrub. Pink/
white/red/yellow fls. in
spring and summer. Size:
up to 10 × 10ft (3 × 3m).

NOMOCHARIS
Liliaceae
Bulb. Pink/white fls. in
mid summer. Size: up to
3ft (90cm). See var.

NEMOPHILA
Hydrophyllaceae
Annual. Blue fls. in
summer. Size: very small.

NICOTIANA
Flowering tobacco
Solanaceae
Annual. White/cream/
pink/purple/greenish fls.
in late summer and
autumn. Size: up to 3 ×
2ft (90 × 60m).

NOTHOFAGUS
Southern beech
Fagaceae
Deciduous and evergreen
tree and shrub. Autumn
colour (if deciduous). Size:
up to 50 × 30ft (15 ×
9m). See var.

NEPETA
incl. Catmint, Ground ivy
Labiatae
Evergreen and semi-
evergreen herbaceous
perennial, spreading
ground-cover. Lavender/
blue/yellow fls. in
summer. Size: up to 2ft
(60cm). See var.

NIEREMBERGIA
Cup flower, White-cup
Solanaceae
Rock plant and annual.
White/mauve/purple/blue
fls. in summer. Size: up to
2ft (60cm). See var.

NOTHOLIRION
Liliaceae
Bulb. Lilac fls. from spring
to late summer. Size: up to
4ft (1.2m).

NERINE
incl. Guernsey lily
Amaryllydaceae
Bulb. Red/pink/white fls.
from late summer to
autumn. Size: up to 2ft
(60cm). See var.

NIGELLA
Love-in-a-mist
Ranunculaceae
Annual. Blue/white/pink/
mauve fls. in summer.
Size: up to 2ft (60cm).

NYMPHAEA
Water lily
Nymphaeaceae
Rhizomatous or tuberous
deciduous herbaceous
perennial deep-water
plant. Most colours all
summer. Size: see var.

NYMPHOIDES
Water fringe/snowflake
Menyanthaceae (sometimes classed in *Gentianaceae*)
Deciduous perennial deep water plant. Yellow fls. in summer. Size: ht. very small, spr. up to 2ft (60cm).

OLEARIA
incl. Daisy bush, Tree aster
Compositae
Evergreen shrub and small tree. White/yellow/red/pink/mauve/purple/blue fls. in spring to autumn. Size: up to 15 × 15ft (4.5 × 4.5m). See var.

ONOPORDUM
incl. Scotch/Cotton/Heraldic thistle
Compositae
Perennial, biennial and annual. Purple fls. in mid summer. Size: 8 × 2½ft (2.5m × 75cm).

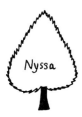

NYSSA
Tupelo, Black gum
Nyssaceae
Deciduous tree. Autumn colour. Size: at maturity 80ft (25m) or more.

OMPHALODES
Navelwort
Boraginaceae
Evergreen and deciduous carpeting rock plant. Blue/white fls. in spring and summer. Size: very small.

ONOSMA
Golden drop
Boraginaceae
Evergreen sub-shrub, perennial, semi-evergreen biennial and annual. Yellow fls. from spring to mid summer. Size: very small.

OENOTHERA
incl. Evening primrose, Dwarf/Ozark snowdrop
Onagraceae
Herbaceous perennial, annual and rock plant. Yellow fls. from spring to autumn. Size: up to 3 × 1ft (90 × 30cm). See var.

ONOCLEA
incl. Sensitive/Bead fern
Polypodiaceae
Rhizomatous herbaceous perennial fern. Size: 2 × 3ft (60 × 90cm).

OPHIOPOGON
incl. Lily-turf, Mondo grass
Liliaceae
Evergreen perennial. White/violet/purple-pink fls. in summer, then frs. Size: up to 2 × 2ft (60 × 60cm).

OLEA
Olive
Oleaceae
Evergreen tree. Foliage and edible frs. Size: up to 30 × 30ft (9 × 9m).

ONONIS
Leguminosae
Deciduous shrub and sub-shrub. Pinkish-purple fls. in mid summer. Size: 2 × 3ft (60 × 90cm).

OPLOPANAX
Devil's club
Araliaceae
Deciduous suckering shrub. Greenish-white fls. in late summer, red frs. Size: 10 × 6ft (3 × 1.8m).

ORCHIS
Orchid
Orchidaceae
Herbaceous perennial.
Lilac/purple/maroon/
pink/red fls., some spotted,
from early to mid summer.
Size: up to $2\frac{1}{2}$ × 1ft (75 ×
30cm).

OSMANTHUS
Sweet olive
Oleaceae
Evergreen shrub and tree.
White/cream fls. in spring
or early autumn. Size:
15 × 15ft (4.5 × 4.5m).

OSTRYA
Hop hornbeam, Ironwood
Carpinaceae (sometimes
classed in *Betulaceae*)
Deciduous tree. Foliage,
catkins, frs. Size: 25 ×
20ft (7.5 × 6m).

ORIGANUM
Common or wild
    marjoram
Labiatae
Mat-forming, sub-shrubby
deciduous perennial
aromatic culinary herb.
Rosy pink/purple fls. in
mid summer. Size: small.

× OSMAREA
Oleaceae
Evergreen shrub. White
fls. in spring. Size: 10 ×
1ft (3m × 30cm).

OURISIA
Scrophulariaceae
Evergreen and semi-
evergreen perennial (some
vars. prostrate). White/
pink/red fls. in summer.
Size: small.

ORNITHOGALUM
Star of Bethlehem,
    Chincherinchee
Liliaceae
Bulb. White fls. in spring
or summer. Size: up to
2 × 2ft (60 × 60cm). See
var.

OSMUNDA
Flowering fern,
    Cinnamon/Interrupted/
    Royal fern
Osmundaceae
Herbaceous perennial fern.
Size: up to 6 × 6ft (1.8 ×
1.8m).

OXALIS
Wood sorrel, Scurvy grass,
    Good luck plant
Oxalidaceae
Rhizomatous and tuberous
perennial and semi-
evergreen sub-shrub.
Pink/purple/red/white/
yellow fls. from spring to
late autumn. See var. Size:
very small.

ORONTIUM
Golden club
Araceae
Deciduous perennial deep-
water plant. White-gold fl.
spikes in spring. Size: ht.
up to $1\frac{1}{2}$ft (45cm).

OSTEOSPERMUM
Cape marigold, African
    daisy
Compositae
Sub-shrubby perennial,
annual and rock plant.
Pink/white/rosy-purple fls.
all summer. Size: small.

OXYDENDRUM
Sorrel tree, Sourwood
Ericaceae
Deciduous shrub or tree.
White fls. in late summer,
autumn colour. Size: up to
40 × 15ft (12 × 4.5m).

OZOTHAMNUS
Snow-in-summer,
  Kerosene bush
Compositae
Evergreen shrub. White
fls. in summer. Size up to:
8 × 6ft (2.5 × 1.8m). See
var.

PANCRATIUM
Sea daffodil/lily
Amaryllidaceae
Deciduous and semi-
evergreen bulb. White fls.
in early summer. Size:
small.

PARAHEBE
Scrophulariaceae
Evergreen prostrate sub-
shrub. White fls. veined
pink or mauve in summer.
Size: small and very small.

PACHYSANDRA
incl. Allegheny/Japanese
  spurge
Buxaceae
Evergreen and semi-
evergreen prostrate sub-
shrub. Foliage. Size: small.

PANICUM
Switch grass
Gramineae
Herbaceous perennial
ornamental grass. Tinged-
red fls. in late summer.
Size: up to 5 × 3ft
(1.5m × 90cm).

PARIS
Herb Paris
Trilliaceae (previously
classed in *Liliaceae*)
Rhizomatous (poisonous)
herbaceous perennial.
Yellow-green fls. in spring
and summer, then frs.
Size: small.

PAEONIA
Peony, Tree peony
Paeoniaceae
Shrub, herbaceous
perennial. Most colours
(except blue) in late spring
and early summer. Size: up
to 8 × 8ft (2.5 × 2.5m).
See var.

PAPAVER
Poppy
Papaveraceae
Annual. White/yellow/
pink/apricot/red/purple
and black-blotched fls. in
summer. Size: up to 2½ ×
1½ft (75 × 45cm). See
var.

PAROCHETUS
Shamrock pea
Leguminosae
Evergreen prostrate
perennial. Blue fls. almost
continuously. Size: height
very small, spread
indefinite.

PALIURUS
Christ's/Jerusalem thorn
Rhamnaceae
Deciduous shrub.
Greenish-yellow fls. in
summer, frs. and autumn
colour. Size: up to 12 ×
12ft (3.5 × 3.5m).

PARADISEA
St Bruno lily
Liliaceae
Rhizomatous herbaceous
perennial. White-green fls.
in early summer. Size: 2 ×
1½ft (60 × 45cm).

PARROTIA
Hamamelidaceae
Spreading tree or
suckering shrub. Autumn
colour. Size: 15 × 25ft
(4.5 × 7.5m).

PARROTIOPSIS
Hamamelidaceae
Small tree or shrub.
Autumn colour. Size:
10 × 8ft (3 × 2.5m).

PAULOWNIA
Foxglove tree, Princess
tree
Bignoniaceae
Deciduous tree. Violet fls.
in spring. Size: at maturity
30 × 30ft (9 × 9m).

PELTIPHYLLUM
Umbrella plant
Saxifragaceae
Bog plant. White-pink fls.
in spring. Size: up to 5 ×
2ft (1.5m × 60cm), also
dwarf.

PARTHENOCISSUS
Boston ivy, Virginia
creeper
Vitaceae
Deciduous self-clinging
climbing shrub. Autumn
colour. Size: up to 70ft
(20m). See var.

PAXISTIMA
Celastraceae
Evergreen low-growing
shrub. Foliage. Size: up to
2 × 5ft (60cm × 1.5m).
See var.

PENNISETUM
incl. Rose fountain grass,
Feathertop
Gramineae
Herbaceous perennial
ornamental grass. Size: up
to 3 × 2ft (90 × 60cm).
See var.

PASSIFLORA
Passionflower
Passifloraceae
Evergreen and semi-
evergreen tendrilled
woody climber. Many
multi-coloured fls. in
summer to autumn; some
vars. produce passionfruit.
Size: up to 30ft (9m).

PELARGONIUM
incl. Regal/Zonal/Ivy/
Scented-leaved
geranium
Geraniaceae
Evergreen sub-shrub,
some trailing. White/pink/
orange/red/purple fls.
from late spring to
autumn. Size: up to 5 ×
3ft (1.5m × 90cm).

PENSTEMON
Scrophulariaceae
Semi-evergreen shrub,
mat-forming sub-shrub,
perennial, rock plant and
annual. Red/pink/purple/
lilac-blue/white/yellow fls.
in summer. Size: up to 7 ×
7ft (2 × 2m). See var.

PATRINIA
Valerianaceae
Herbaceous clump-
forming perennial. Yellow
fls. all summer. Size: very
small.

PELTANDRA
White/green water arum
Araceae
Herbaceous perennial
marginal aquatic. Size: ht.
up to 1½ft (45cm).

PERILLA
Labiatae
Annual. White fls. in
summer. Size: 2 × 1ft
(60 × 30cm).

PERNETTYA
Ericaceae
Evergreen shrub. White fls. in spring, white/pink/red/purple frs. Size: 3 × 3ft (90 × 90cm).

PETUNIA
Solanaceae
Annual. Red/purple/blue/pink/yellow/white fls. in summer and autumn. Size: small.

PHILADELPHUS
Mock orange
Philadelphaceae
Deciduous scented shrub. Size: see var.

PEROVSKIA
Russian sage
Labiatae
Deciduous sub-shrub. Blue fls. in late summer. Size: up to 5 × 1½ft (1.5m × 45cm).

PHACELIA
Hydrophyllaceae
Annual. Blue fls. all summer. Size: up to 2 × 1ft (60 × 30cm).

PHILESIA
Liliaceae (sometimes classed in *Philesiaceae*)
Evergreen thicket-forming sometimes climbing shrub. Crimson fls. in mid to late summer. Size: 4 × 4ft (1.2 × 1.2m).

PETROPHYTUM
Rock spiraea, Mock orange
Philadelphaceae
Deciduous scented shrub. Size: see var.

PHALARIS
Gardener's garters, Ribbon grass
Gramineae
Ornamental herbaceous perennial grass. Size: up to 5 × 2ft (1.5m × 60cm).

PHILLYREA
Jasmine box
Oleaceae
Evergreen shrub. Greenish-white fls. in late spring. Size: 10 × 10ft (3 × 3m).

PETRORHAGIA
Tunic flower
Caryophyllaceae
Evergreen prostrate rock plant. Pink/white fls. in summer. Size: very small.

PHELLODENDRON
Amur cork tree
Rutaceae
Evergreen spreading tree. Size: 25 × 30ft (7.5 × 9m).

PHLOMIS
Jerusalem sage
Labiatae
Evergreen shrub. Size: 4 × 3ft (1.2m × 90cm).

PHLOX
Polemoniaceae
Herbaceous or evergreen perennial, hummock-forming or creeping rock plant, annual. For colour, season and size see var. Size: up to 4 × 2ft (1.2m × 60cm).

PHYGELIUS
Cape figwort/fuchsia
Scrophulariaceae
Deciduous wall shrub and sub-shrub. Red fls. in summer. Size: up to 4 × 2ft (1.2m × 60cm).

× PHYLLOTHAMNUS
Ericaceae
Evergreen dense shrublet. Pink fls. in spring. Size: small.

PHORMIUM
New Zealand flax
Agavaceae
Evergreen perennial with brightly coloured sword-like lvs. Size: up to 10ft (3m).

PHYLLITIS
Hart's-tongue fern, Spleenwort
Polypodiaceae
Herbaceous perennial fern. Size: up to 2 × 1ft (60 × 30cm).

PHYSALIS
incl. Chinese lantern, Bladder cherry
Solanaceae
Herbaceous border perennial. Creamy-white fls. in mid summer, orange frs. Size: up to 3ft (90cm).

PHOTINIA
incl. Christmas berry, Stranvaesia
Rosaceae
Evergreen and deciduous shrub and small tree. Young growth colourful, some vars. autumn colour. Size: up to 15 × 15ft (4.5 × 4.5m). See var.

PHYLLODOCE
Mountain heath
Ericaceae
Evergreen compact (some dwarf, mat-forming) shrub. White/blue/purple/red/pink/yellow fls. from spring to summer. Size: small and very small.

PHYSOCARPUS
incl. Ninebark
Rosaceae
Deciduous shrub. White-pink fls. in early summer. Peeling bark. Size: 10 × 10ft (3 × 3m) or more.

PHUOPSIS
Rubiaceae
Perennial ground-cover. Pink fls. in summer. Size: small.

PHYLLOSTACHYS
Bamboo
Gramineae
Evergreen or semi-evergreen woody-stemmed perennial giant grass, clump-forming, with different coloured canes. Size: up to 20ft (6m).

PHYSOPLEXIS
Horned rampion
Campanulaceae
Herbaceous rock plant. Purplish fls. in mid summer. Size: very small.

PHYSOSTEGIA
Obedient plant, Lion's
heart, False dragonhead
Labiatae
Herbaceous perennial.
Mauve/pink/white fls. in
late summer. Size: up to
4 × 2ft (1.2m × 60cm).

PIERIS
Andromeda, Lily-of-the-
valley shrub
Ericaceae
Evergreen shrub. White
fls. in spring, then bs. and
leaf colour. Size: up to
12 × 15ft (3.5 × 4.5m).
See var.

PIPTANTHUS
Evergreen laburnum
Leguminosae
Evergreen wall shrub.
Yellow fls. in late spring.
Size: up to 10 × 10ft (3 ×
3m).

PHYTEUMA
Horned rampion
Campanulaceae
Herbaceous perennial and
rock plant. Blue fls. in
early summer. Size: small.

PILEOSTEGIA
Saxifragaceae
Evergreen self-clinging
woody climber. White fls.
in late summer. Size: up to
25ft (7.5m).

PITTOSPORUM
incl. Tobira, Karo,
Victorian box
Pittosporaceae
Evergreen shrub or small
tree. Red/creamy-white fls.
in late spring. Foliage. Size:
up to 30 × 20ft (9 × 6m).
See var.

PHYTOLACCA
Pokeweed, Pokeberry
Phytolaccaceae
Herbaceous erect
perennial. Greenish-white/
pink fls. in summer. Lvs./
stem autumn colour. Size:
up to 10 × 3ft (3m ×
90cm). See var.

PINELLIA
Araceae
Rhizomatous plant.
Greenish-purple spathes in
late summer. Size: very
small.

PLAGIANTHUS
Hoheria, Lacebark
Malvaceae
Evergreen or deciduous
tree and shrub. Whitish
fls. from mid to late
summer. Size: up to 8 ×
12ft (2.5 × 3.5m).

PICEA
Spruce, Fir, Hemlock
Pinaceae
Coniferous tree, erect and
weeping. Size: at maturity
up to 115ft (35m). See
var.

PINUS
Pine
Pinaceae
Evergreen coniferous tree,
conical, round or flat-
headed, also prostrate and
dwarf vars. Size: at
maturity 100ft (30m) or
more. See var.

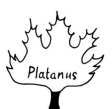

PLATANUS
Plane tree, Sycamore
Platanaceae
Deciduous tree. Size: at
maturity 100ft (30m) or
more. See var.

PLATYCODON
Balloon flower
Campanulaceae
Herbaceous clump-forming perennial. White/mauve/blue/pink fls. all summer. Size: 3 × 1½ft (90 × 45cm).

PODOCARPUS
Podocarp, Plum-fruited/Chilean/Southern/Japanese yew, New Zealand white/Yew pine, Alpine totara
Podocarpaceae
Evergreen shrub or tree. Size: at maturity up to 50ft (15m). See var.

POLYGALA
Milkwort, Ground box
Polygalaceae
Evergreen mat-forming rock plant. Blue/yellow/cream/red/yellow fls. from spring to early summer. Size: small.

PLATYSTEMON
Cream cups
Papaveraceae
Annual. Creamy-yellow/pink-green fls. in early summer. Size: small.

PODOPHYLLUM
May apple, Himalayan mayflower
Berberidaceae
Herbaceous low-growing perennial. White/blue/pink fls. in early summer, then frs. Size: small.

POLYGONATUM
Solomon's seal
Liliaceae
Rhizomatous herbaceous perennial. White fls. in late spring. Size: up to 6 × 2½ft (1.8m × 75cm). See var.

PLEIOBLASTUS
Arundinaria, Bamboo
Gramineae
Evergreen perennial giant grass or bamboo. Size: up to 2 × 4ft (60cm × 1.2m).

POLEMONIUM
Jacob's ladder, Greek valerian
Polemoniaceae
Herbaceous perennial. White/violet-blue/pink fls. from late spring to late summer. Size: up to 2½ × 1½ft (75 × 45cm).

POLYGONUM
Russian/Mile-a-minute vine, Chinese/Bokhara fleece flower, Knotweed
Polygonaceae
Deciduous climber, annual, herbaceous perennial and rock plant. White/pink/red fls. from summer to autumn. Size: up to 40ft (12m). See var.

PLUMBAGO
Cape leadwort/plumbago
Plumbaginaceae
Semi-evergreen bushy perennial, climber and herbaceous perennial. Blue fls. all summer. Size: up to 12ft (3.5m). See var.

POLIANTHES
Tuberose
Agavaceae
Rhizomatous plant. White fls. from late summer to autumn. Size: up to 3½ft (1.1m).

POLYPODIUM
Common polypody
Polypodiaceae
Evergreen creeping fern. Size: small.

POLYSTICHUM
Japanese holly fern
Polypodiaceae
Evergreen perennial fern.
Size: up to 3 × 3ft (90 ×
90cm).

PONCIRUS
Hardy or trifoliate/
  Japanese bitter orange
Rutaceae
Deciduous shrub. White
fls. in late spring. Size:
10 × 10ft (3 × 3m).

PONTEDERIA
Pickerel weed
Pontederiaceae
Rhizomatous marginal
aquatic. Blue fls. in late
summer. Size: ht. up to 5ft
(1.5m). See var.

POPULUS
Poplar, incl. Abele, Balm
  of Gilead, Black
  cottonwood
Salicaceae
Deciduous tree. Size: up to
60ft (18m). See var.

POTENTILLA
incl. Shrubby cinquefoil,
  Buttercup shrub, Five
  finger
Rosaceae
Deciduous shrub, rock
plant and herbaceous
perennial. Yellow/white/
red/pink/orange fls. from
spring to autumn. Size: up
to 4 × 4ft (1.2 × 1.2m).

PRIMULA
incl. Primrose, Cowslip,
  Auricula, Polyanthus
Primulaceae
Perennial and rock plant.
Most colours, mainly from
spring to early summer.
Size: up to 2ft (60cm).

PROSTANTHERA
Mint bush
Labiatae
Evergreen shrub. Lilac to
blue-purple fls. in spring.
Size: 5 × ft (1.5 × 1.5m).

PRUNELLA
Self-heal
Labiatae
Deciduous spreading rock
plant. Pink/purple/white
fls. all summer. Size: small.

PRUNUS
incl. Almond, Apricot,
  Cherry, Damson, Plum,
  Greengage, Peach
Rosaceae
Deciduous fruit tree and
shrub. Pink/white/red fls.
in winter and early spring,
frs. and autumn colour.
Size: up to 36 × 20ft
(11 × 6m).

PSEUDOLARIX
Golden larch
Pinaceae
Deciduous pyramid-
shaped tree. Autumn
colour. Size: 50ft (15m).

PSEUDOPANAX
Lancewood
Araliaceae
Evergreen tree. Size: 15 ×
7ft (4.5 × 2m).

PSEUDOTSUGA
Douglas fir
Pinaceae
Evergreen coniferous tree
and low growing bush.
Size: at maturity 160ft
(50m). See var.

PSEUDOWINTERA
Winter's bark, Mountain
 pepper tree
Winteraceae
Evergreen tree and shrub.
Size: up to 25 × 15ft
(7.5 × 4.5m). See var.

PTEROCEPHALUS
Dipsacaceae
Evergreen cushion-
forming rock plant.
Purplish-pink fls. in
summer. Size: very small.

PULSATILLA
Pasque flower
Ranunculaceae
Dwarf perennial rock
plant. White/yellow/pink/
red/blue fls. in late spring.
Size: small.

PSYLLOSTACHYS
Statice, Sea lavender
Plumbaginaceae
Annual. Yellow/white/
blue/purple/red/pink fls.
from mid summer. Size:
small.

PTEROSTYRAX
Epaulette tree
Styracaceae
Deciduous shrub or small
tree. Creamy-white fls. in
early summer. Size: 20 ×
18ft (6 × 5.5m).

PUSCHKINIA
Striped squill
Liliaceae
Bulb. Blue/white fls. in
spring. Size: very small.

PTELEA
Hop tree
Rutaceae
Deciduous tree and shrub.
Size: up to 22 × 22ft (7 ×
7m).

PTILOTRICHUM
Spiny alyssum
Cruciferae
Evergreen sub-shrub.
Creamy-white fls. in early
summer. Size: very small.

PYRACANTHA
Firethorn
Rosaceae
Evergreen shrub, wall
shrub and semi-prostrate
var. White fls. in early
summer, bright-coloured
frs. Size: up to 10 × 10ft
(3 × 3m).

PTEROCARYA
Wing nut
Juglandaceae
Deciduous tree. Size: 33 ×
30ft (10 × 9m).

PULMONARIA
incl. Lungwort, Jerusalem
 cowslip, Jerusalem/
 Bethlehem sage,
 Soldiers and sailors,
 Spotted dog
Boraginaceae
Evergreen perennial
ground-cover. White/
blue/pink/purple/fls. in
late spring. Size: small.

PYROLA
Wintergreen
Pyrolaceae
Evergreen mat-forming
perennial. Greenish-white/
pinkish-purple fls. in mid
summer. Size: small.

PYRUS
Ornamental pear
Rosaceae
Evergreen shrub. Size up
to 25ft (7.5m).

REHDERODENDRON
Styracaceae
Deciduous small tree.
Creamy-white fls. in late
spring. Size: 20 × 10ft
(6 × 3m).

RHAZYA
Periwinkle
Apocynaceae
Herbaceous perennial.
Blue fls. in summer. Size:
small.

QUERCUS
Oak
Fagaceae
Deciduous and evergreen
tree and shrub. Size: at
maturity up to 100ft
(30m). See var.

RESEDA
Mignonette
Resedaceae
Annual. Yellowish-reddish
fls. in summer. Size: small.

RHEUM
Ornamental rhubarb
Polygonaceae
Herbaceous perennial.
Yellow/pink/red fls. in late
spring and bright-coloured
lvs. Size: up to 7ft (2m).
See var.

RAMONDA
Gesneriaceae
Evergreen rock plant.
Blue/white/pink/lilac fls.
in spring. Size: very small.

RHAMNUS
Buckthorn
Rhamnaceae
Evergreen and deciduous
shrub. Foliage. Size: up to
15 × 12ft (4.5 × 3.5m).
See var.

RHODODENDRON
incl. Azalea
Ericaceae
Evergreen and deciduous
flowering shrub and tree.
All colours except true
blue. See var. for colour,
season and size.

RANUNCULUS
Fair maids of France/Kent,
Lesser celandine, Great
spearwort
Ranunculaceae
Herbaceous perennial,
alpine, tuberous marginal
aquatic. White/yellow/
orange/pink/red fls. in
summer. Size: up to 3 ×
2ft (90 × 60cm).

RHAPHIOLEPIS
incl. Indian hawthorn
Rosaceae
Evergreen shrub and small
tree. Pink/white fls. in
spring or summer. Size:
5 × 6ft (1.5 × 1.8m). See
var.

RHODOTYPOS
Jetbead, White kerria
Rosaceae
Deciduous shrub. White
fls. in late spring and
summer. Size: up to 5 ×
7ft (1.5 × 2m).

RHUS
Sumach, Nutgall, Varnish
  tree, Wax tree, Poison
  oak
Anacardiaceae
Deciduous suckering
shrub (some vars.
poisonous). Autumn
colour. Size: up to 25 ×
25ft (7.5 × 7.5m). See
var.

ROBINIA
Locust, Acacia, False
  acacia
Leguminosae
Deciduous tree and shrub.
Pink/lavender/white fls. in
early summer. Size: up to
40 × 30ft (12 × 9m). See
var.

ROSA
Rose
Rosaceae
Deciduous shrub, rambler
and climber. Most colours
(except blue) from spring
to early winter: some vars.
have hips. Size: see var.

RIBES
Flowering currant and
  gooseberry
Grossulariaceae
Deciduous and evergreen
shrub. Pink/yellow/
crimson/red fls. in spring
and early summer, frs.
Size: up to 7 × 8ft (2 ×
2.5m). See var.

RODGERSIA
Saxifragaceae
Perennial. Cream/pink/
white fls. from early to mid
summer. Size: up to 6 ×
2½ft (1.8m × 75cm).

ROSMARINUS
Rosemary
Labiatae
Evergreen erect and
prostrate bushy shrub,
dwarf vars. for ground-
cover. Blue/mauve fls. in
spring and summer. Size:
up to 7 × 7ft (2 × 2m).
See var.

RICHEA
Epacridaceae
Evergreen shrub. White/
pink/red fls. in late spring.
Size: 5 × 3ft (1.5m ×
90cm) or more.

ROMNEYA
Matilija/California tree
  poppy
Papaveraceae
Herbaceous sub-shrubby
perennial. White fls. in
mid summer. Size: up to
3 × 10ft (90cm × 3m).

RUBUS
incl. Bramble, Blackberry,
  Loganberry, Raspberry
Rosaceae
Deciduous, semi-evergreen
and evergreen shrub,
scrambling climber.
White/pink/red/purple fls.
in early summer, frs. Size:
up to 10 × 15ft (3 ×
4.5m). See var.

RICINUS
Castor bean, Castor oil
  plant
Euphorbiaceae
Poisonous tender tree
grown as annual for
foliage. Size: 15ft (4.5m).

ROMULEA
Iridaceae
Corm. Purple/violet fls. in
early spring. Size: very
small.

RUDBECKIA
Coneflower
Compositae
Herbaceous perennial and
annual. Yellow fls. from
mid to late summer. Size:
up to 3 × 1½ft (90 ×
45cm).

RUSCUS
Butcher's broom, Box
    holly
Liliaceae
Evergreen erect, clump-
forming and carpeting
shrub. Red bs. Size: up to
3 × 3ft (90 × 90cm). See
var.

SALIX
Willow, Osier
Salicaceae
Deciduous upright and
weeping tree and shrub,
creeping alpine. Catkins.
Size: up to 40 × 25ft
(12 × 7.5m). See var.

SANGUINARIA
Bloodroot
Papaveraceae
Rhizomatous herbaceous
perennial rock plant.
White fls. in spring. Size:
small.

RUTA
Rue, Herb of grace
Rutaceae
Evergreen shrub. Foliage
and greenish-yellow fls.
from early to mid summer.
Size: 3 × 2ft (90 ×
60cm).

SALPIGLOSSIS
Painted tongue, Velvet
    flower
Solanaceae
Annual. Most colours in
summer and early
autumn. Size: 2½ × 1ft
(75 × 30cm).

SANGUISORBA
Burnet
Rosaceae
Perennial. White/pink fls.
in summer. Size: up to 6 ×
2ft (1.8m × 60cm). See
var.

SAGINA
Pearlwort
Caryophyllaceae
Mossy matting rock plant.
White fls. in early
summer. Size: very small.

SALVIA
Sage
Labiatae
Evergreen and semi-
evergreen shrub, sub-
shrub, perennial and
annual. Some coloured
lvs, red/purple/blue/pink/
white fls. in summer. Size:
up to 5 × 2ft (1.5m ×
60cm). See var.

SANTOLINA
Cotton lavender
Compositae
Evergreen shrub. Yellow/
cream fls. in summer. Size:
up to 2½ × 3ft (75 ×
90cm). See var.

SAGITTARIA
Water plantain,
    Arrowhead
Alismataceae
Tuberous herbaceous
perennial marginal
aquatic. White fls. in
summer: edible tubers.
Size: up to 2½ × 3ft (75 ×
90cm).

SAMBUCUS
Elder
Caprifoliaceae (sometimes
classed in *Sambucaceae*)
Deciduous shrub and tree.
Foliage and berries.
Creamy-white fls. in early
summer. Size: up to 15 ×
15ft (4.5 × 4.5m). See
var.

SANVITALIA
Creeping zinnia
Compositae
Perennial, trailing annual.
Yellow fls. in summer.
Size: very small.

SAPONARIA
Soapwort, Bouncing Bet
Caryophyllaceae
Perennial, annual and
prostrate and trailing rock
plant. Pink/white fls. from
early to late summer. Size:
3 × 2ft (90 × 60cm). See
var.

SATUREJA
Winter savory
Labiatae
Semi-evergreen perennial,
sub-shrub and annual.
Pink fls. in early summer.
Size: small.

SCHISANDRA
Magnolia vine
Schisandraceae (formerly
classed in *Magnoliaceae*)
Deciduous perennial
twining climber. White/
pink/red/orange fls. in
spring, then frs. Size: up to
30ft (9m). See var.

SARCOCOCCA
Christmas/Sweet box
Buxaceae
Evergreen shrub. White
fls. in late winter, then bs.
Size: up to 4 × 2ft
(1.2m × 60cm). See var.

SAXEGOTHAEA
Prince Albert yew
Podocarpaceae
Evergreen coniferous tree,
conical, weeping or bushy
acc. to climate. Size: at
maturity up to 50 × 15ft
(15 × 4.5m).

SCHIZANTHUS
Butterfly flower, Poor
    man's orchid
Solanaceae
Annual. Pink/purple/red/
white fls. in summer and
autumn. Size: up to 3 ×
1ft (90 × 30cm).

SASA
Bamboo
Gramineae (sometimes
classed in *Bambusoideae*)
Evergreen perennial giant
grass, also dwarf vars.
Size: up to 8ft (2.5m).

SAXIFRAGA
London pride, Mother of
    thousands, Fair maids of
    France, Strawberry
    geranium
Saxifragaceae
Evergreen, semi-evergreen
perennial and rock plant.
White/yellow/pink/red fls.
from late spring. Size:
small.

SCHIZOPHRAGMA
incl. Japanese hydrangea
    vine
Hydrangeaceae
Deciduous self-clinging
woody climber. White/
cream/pink fls. in early
summer. Size: up to 40ft
(12m). See var.

SASSAFRAS
Lauraceae
Deciduous shrub or
conical tree. Size: up to
25 × 12ft (7.5 × 3.5m).

SCABIOSA
Pincushion flower
Dipsacaceae
Perennial (some
evergreen), annual and
rock plant. Blue/white/
mauve/red/yellow/pink
fls. in late spring and
summer. Size: up to 3 ×
1ft (90 × 30cm). See var.

SCHIZOSTYLIS
Kaffir lily, Crimson flag
Iridaceae
Rhizomatous perennial.
Crimson/pink fls. in
autumn. Size: up to 2½ft
(75cm).

SCIADOPITYS
Umbrella pine
Taxodiaceae (sometimes classed in *Pinaceae*)
Coniferous pyramidal tree. Size: at maturity 30 × 16ft (9 × 5m).

SCILLA
Squill
Liliaceae
Bulb. Blue/white/pink fls. in late spring. Size: very small.

SCIRPUS
Sedge, Round-headed/ Bristle club/Zebra rush
Cyperaceae
Evergreen perennial and annual marginal aquatic rush. Foliage. Size: up to 3ft (90cm).

SCUTELLARIA
Skullcap
Labiatae
Rhizomatous deciduous perennial, upright and mat-forming rock plant. White/purple-blue fls. in summer. Size: very small.

SEDUM
incl. Donkey's tail, Rose-root, Stonecrop
Crassulaceae
Evergreen succulent perennial, sub-shrub and rock plant. Pink/red/ yellow/orange/white/ purple fls. from spring to autumn. Size: up to 3 × 2ft (90 × 60cm). See var.

SELINUM
Himalayan parsley
Umbelliferae
Herbaceous perennial. White fls. in summer. Size: up to 5 × 2ft (1.5m × 60cm).

SEMIAQUILEGIA
Ranunculaceae
Perennial rock plant. Red-purple fls. in late spring. Size: small.

SEMPERVIVUM
Houseleek
Crassulaceae
Evergreen succulent hummock/mat-forming rock plant. Yellow/pink/ red/purple/fls. in mid summer. Size: very small.

SENECIO
incl. Silver-leaved cineraria, Dusty miller
Compositae
Evergreen shrub, sub-shrub, twining climber, perennial and annual. Yellow/pink/red/purple/ blue fls. all summer. Size: up to 7 × 3ft (2m × 90cm). See var.

SEQUOIA/ SEQUOIADENDRON
incl. Redwood, Californian big tree, Giant sequoia, Wellingtonia
Taxodiaceae
Coniferous tree, weeping, bushy, prostrate vars. of the world's tallest tree. Size: up to 330ft (100m). See var.

SERRATULA
Compositae
Herbaceous thistly perennial. Purple fls. in late summer. Size: very small.

SHEPHERDIA
Buffalo berry
Elaeagnaceae
Deciduous or evergreen shrub. Foliage, bs. Size: 10 × 7ft (3 × 2m).

SHIBATAEA
Bamboo
Gramineae (sometimes classed in *Bambusoideae*)
Evergreen and semi-evergreen perennial compact grass (bamboo).
Size: to 2½ft (75cm).

SINARUNDINARIA
Bamboo
Gramineae (sometimes classed in *Bambusoideae*)
Evergreen and semi-evergreen perennial grass.
Size: up to 13ft (4m).

SOLANUM
Potato bush/vine, Jasmine nightshade
Solanaceae
Semi-evergreen shrub and herbaceous woody climber. Blue fls. in summer and autumn. Size: up to 20ft (6m). See var.

SIDALCEA
Chequer mallow
Malvaceae
Herbaceous perennial. Pink/crimson fls. all summer. Size: up to 4 × 1½ft (1.2m × 45cm).

SISYRINCHIUM
Blue-eyed/Golden-eyed grass, Grass widow
Iridaceae
Evergreen and deciduous perennial, tufty rock plant. Creamy-yellow/white/violet/purple fls. from spring to autumn. Size: 2 × 1ft (60 × 30cm).

SOLEIROLIA
Mind-your-own-business, Baby's tears, Mother of thousands
Urticaceae
Evergreen perennial carpeting plant. Foliage. Size: very small.

SILENE
Campion, Catchfly, Cushion pink
Caryophyllaceae
Evergreen and deciduous perennial, annual, biennial, mat-forming rock plant. Pink/white/purple/blue fls. from spring to autumn. Size: small.

SKIMMIA
Rutaceae
Evergreen low-growing shrub. White/pink/yellow fls. in spring then frs. Size: 3 × 5ft (90cm × 1.5m). See var.

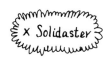

SOLIDAGO
Golden rod
Compositae
Herbaceous perennial and rock plant. Yellow fls. from mid summer to autumn. Size: 6 × 2½ft (1.8m × 75cm). See var.

SILYBUM
Blessed/Our lady's milk/St Mary's thistle
Compositae
Thistly biennial. Violet fls. in summer. Size: 4 × 2ft (1.2m × 60cm).

SMILACINA
False Solomon's seal, False spikenard, Star-flowered lily-of-the-valley
Liliaceae
Rhizomatous herbaceous perennial. White/cream/pink fls. in late spring, then bs. Size: 3 × 1½ft (90 × 45cm). See var.

× **SOLIDASTER**
Compositae
Herbaceous perennial. Yellow fls. in mid summer. Size: 2½ × 1ft (75 × 30cm).

SOPHORA
incl. Japanese/Weeping
   pagoda tree, Chinese
   scholar tree, Kowhai
Leguminosae
Semi-evergreen and
deciduous tree and shrub.
Yellow/creamy-white/
violet-blue fls. in spring
and early summer. Size: up
to 65ft (20m). See var.

SORBARIA
False spirea
Rosaceae
Deciduous shrub. White
fls. in mid summer. Size:
up to 8 × 8ft (2.5 ×
2.5m). See var.

SORBUS
incl. Mountain ash,
   Rowan, Whitebeam,
   Wild service tree
Rosaceae
Deciduous tree and shrub.
Generally white fls. in
spring, frs. late summer
and autumn colour. Size:
up to 25 × 18ft (7.5 ×
5.5m). See var.

SPARAXIS
Harlequin/Wand flower
Iridaceae
Herbaceous corm. White/
yellow/orange/red fls.
from late spring. Size:
small.

SPARTINA
Variegated cord grass
Gramineae
Herbaceous perennial
ornamental grass. Size: up
to 6 × 3ft (1.8m ×
90cm).

SPARTIUM
Spanish broom
Leguminosae
Deciduous shrub. Yellow
fls. all summer. Size: 10 ×
8ft (3 × 2.5m).

SPIRAEA
Foam of May, Bridal
   wreath
Rosaceae
Deciduous shrub. White/
pink fls. in late spring and
early summer. Size: up to
7 × 8ft (2 × 2.5m). See
var.

STACHYS
Betony, Bishop's-wort,
   Lamb's tongue/ear
Labiatae
Herbaceous and evergreen
mat-forming perennial.
Foliage and pink/purple
fls. early to late summer.
Size: up to 3 × 1ft (90 ×
30cm). See var.

STACHYURUS
Stachyuraceae
Deciduous shrub. Yellow
fls. in early spring. Size:
7 × 7ft (2 × 2m).

STATICE
Sea lavender
Plumbaginaceae
Evergreen perennial,
annual and biennial. Fls.
most colours in summer.
Size: up to 2 × 3ft (60 ×
90cm).

STEPHANANDRA
Rosaceae
Deciduous shrub.
Greenish/creamy-white
fls. in early summer. Some
vars. autumn colour. Size:
5 × 8ft (1.5 × 2.5m).

STERNBERGIA
incl. Autumn or Winter
   daffodil (may be biblical
   Lily of the field)
Amaryllidaceae
Bulb. Yellow fls. from
spring to autumn. Size:
very small.

STEWARTIA
Theaceae
Deciduous tree and shrub. Creamy-white fls. in summer. Peeling bark and autumn colour. Size: up to 50ft (15m). See var.

STRATIOTES
Water soldier
Hydrocharitaceae
Deep water floating plant. White fls. in summer. Size: very small.

SYMPHORICARPOS
Snowberry, Coral berry, Indian currant
Caprifoliaceae
Deciduous shrub, thicket-forming and ground-cover. Pink/white fls. in summer, coloured frs. Size: 7 × 10ft (2 × 3m). See var.

STIPA
Feather or Needle grass
Gramineae
Herbaceous perennial tufted ornamental grass. Size: up to 7 × 3ft (2m × 90cm). See var.

STYLOPHORUM
Celandine/Wood poppy
Papaveraceae
Herbaceous perennial. Yellow fls. in late spring. Size: small.

SYMPHYTUM
Comfrey, Boneset
Boraginaceae
Perennial for ground-cover. Cream/yellow/white/pink/red/purple/blue fls. from spring to summer. Size: up to 4 × 4ft (1.2 × 1.2m). See var.

STOKESIA
Stoke's/Cornflower aster
Compositae
Herbaceous perennial. White/pink/blue fls. in late summer and autumn. Size: small.

STYRAX
Storax, Snowbell
Styracaceae
Deciduous small spreading tree and shrub. White fls. in early summer. Size: up to 20 × 20ft (6 × 6m). See var.

SYMPLOCOS
Asiatic sweetleaf
Symplocaceae
Deciduous shrub or small tree. White fls. in late spring, then frs. Size: 8 × 7ft (2.5 × 2m).

STRANVAESIA
Rosaceae
Evergreen shrub and small tree. White fls. in early summer, frs. and autumn colour. Size: 10 × 10ft (3 × 3m).

SYCOPSIS
Hamamelidaceae
Evergreen shrub or small tree. Reddish-yellow fls. in spring. Size: 10 × 7ft (3 × 2m).

SYRINGA
Lilac
Oleaceae
Deciduous suckering shrub, some tree-like. White/creamy-yellow/pink/red/mauve/purple fls. in late spring. Size: up to 30 × 15ft (9 × 4.5m). See var.

TAGETES
Marigold
Compositae
Annual. Red/yellow/white fls. in summer and autumn. Size: up to 3 × 1½ft (90 × 45cm). See var.

TAXUS
Yew
Taxaceae
Evergreen bushy tree and shrub: columnar, tiered and prostrate vars. Size: up to 40ft (12m). See var.

THELYPTERIS
incl. Broad/Beech/Marsh/ New York ferns
Polypodiaceae
Rhizomatous fern. Size: up to 2 × 2ft (60 × 60cm).

TAMARIX
Tamarisk
Tamaricaceae
Deciduous shrub or small tree. Pink fls. in late summer. Size: up to 15 × 15ft (4.5 × 4.5m). See var.

TELLIMA
Fringecup
Saxifragaceae
Semi-evergreen perennial. Greenish-white turning red/purple fls. in late spring. Size: 2 × 2ft (60 × 60cm).

THUJA/THUJOPSIS
incl. Arbor-vitae, Northern white/Western red cedar
Cupressaceae
Evergreen coniferous tree and dwarf shrub. Size: up to 100ft (30m). See var.

TANACETUM
Compositae
Deciduous and evergreen erect and mat-forming perennial and sub-shrub. Silver foliage. Pink/white/ yellow/beige fls. in summer. Size: up to 3 × 1½ft (90 × 45cm). See var.

TEUCRIUM
Shrubby germander
Labiatae
Evergreen shrub. Purple/ lavender/blue fls. in summer. Size: 5 × 4ft (1.5 × 1.2m).

THUNBERGIA
incl. Clock vine, Black-eyed Susan
Acanthaceae
Evergreen woody perennial and annual twining climber. Purplish-blue/orange/yellow/white fls. in spring and summer. Size: up to 20ft (6m). See var.

TAXODIUM
Swamp or Bald cypress
Taxodiaceae
Deciduous coniferous conical tree. Size: up to 36 × 16ft (11 × 5m). See var.

THALICTRUM
Meadow rue
Ranunculaceae
Herbaceous perennial and rock plant. Lilac/purple/ yellow/white fls. from early summer. Size: up to 6 × 2ft (1.8m × 60cm). See var.

THYMUS
Thyme
Labiatae
Evergreen perennial culinary herb, mat-forming rock plant. Pink/ lilac/white fls. in early summer. Size: small and very small.

TIARELLA
Foam flower
Saxifragaceae
Semi-evergreen perennial.
White/pink fls. from late
spring. Size: small.

TOLMIEA
Piggy-back plant
Saxifragaceae
Evergreen perennial
ground-cover. Size: very
small.

TRACHYSTEMON
Eastern borage
Boraginaceae
Perennial ground-cover.
Blue fls. in spring. Size:
small.

TIGRIDIA
Tiger flower, Shell flower
Iridaceae
Herbaceous bulb. White/
yellow/orange/lilac/red
fls. from mid summer. Size:
small.

TRACHELOSPERMUM
Star/Confederate jasmine
Apocynaceae
Evergreen perennial
twining woody climber.
Yellow/white/cream fls. in
summer. Size: up to 25ft
(7.5m).

TRADESCANTIA
incl. Spiderwort, Trinity
    flower, Wandering Jew,
    Boat lily, Moses-in-the-
    cradle
Commelinaceae
Deciduous and evergreen
perennial. Pink-purple/
blue/red/white fls. from
late spring. Size: up to 3 ×
2ft (90 × 60cm). See var.

TILIA
Lime, Linden, Basswood
Tiliaceae
Deciduous erect and
weeping tree. Size: up to
100ft (30m). See var.

TRACHYCARPUS
Windmill/Chusana palm
Palmae
Palm tree. Size: 10 × 8ft
(3 × 2.5m).

TRICYRTIS
Toad lily
Liliaceae
Rhizomatous herbaceous
perennial. White/yellow-
cream fls. in early autumn.
Size: up to 3 × 2ft (90 ×
60cm). See var.

TITHONIA
Mexican sunflower
Compositae
Annual. Orange-red fls. in
summer. Size: 4 × 3ft
(1.2m × 90cm).

TRACHYMENE
Blue lace flower
Umbelliferae
Annual. Lavender-blue fls.
in summer. Size: small.

TRILLIUM
incl. Wood lily, Wake
    robin, Nodding trillium,
    Toadshade, Painted lady
Trilliaceae
Rhizomatous herbaceous
perennial. White/pink/
maroon/yellow/cream/red
fls. in spring. Size: up to
$2\frac{1}{2}$ × 1ft (75 × 30cm).
See var.

TRITELEIA
Wild hyacinth
Liliaceae/Alliaceae
Herbaceous perennial
corm. White/lilac-blue/
yellow fls. in spring and
early summer. Size: small.

TSUGA
Hemlock
Pinaceae
Evergreen coniferous tree
and prostrate, carpet-
forming dwarf vars. Size:
up to 100ft (30m). See
var.

UMBELLULARIA
Headache tree, California
laurel/bay
Lauraceae
Evergreen tree or shrub.
Size: up to 25 × 25ft
(7.5 × 7.5m).

TRITONIA
Iridaceae
Herbaceous corm. Pink/
orange/yellow/cream/
white fls. in late spring.
Size: small.

TULIPA
Tulip
Liliaceae
Bulb. Most colours (except
blue), many multi- and
bicoloured fls. in spring.
Size: small.

URSINIA
Compositae
Annual. Yellow fls. in
summer. Size: small.

TROLLIUS
Globe flower
Ranunculaceae
Herbaceous perennial and
rock plant. Yellow-orange
fls. in early summer. Size:
up to 3 × 1½ft (90 ×
30cm). See var.

TYPHA
Reedmace, Cat-tail
Typhaceae
Rhizomatous herbaceous
perennial grass-like
marginal aquatic. Size: up
to 6ft (1.8m).

UVULARIA
Merrybell, Bellwort
Liliaceae
Herbaceous perennial.
Yellow fls. in late spring.
Size: small.

TROPAEOLUM
Perennial nasturtium,
  Indian cress, Flame/
  Canary creeper
Tropaeolaceae
Tuberous herbaceous
perennial climber, annual
and trailing, prostrate rock
plant. Red/orange/yellow
fls. in summer. Size: up to
15ft (4.5m). See var.

ULMUS
Elm
Ulmaceae
Deciduous and semi-
evergreen tree and shrub.
Size: up to 120ft (36.5m).
See var.

VACCINIUM
incl. Blueberry, Bilberry,
  Whortleberry,
  European/Small
  cranberry
Ericaceae
Evergreen and deciduous
shrub, creeping dwarf vars.
White/pink/red fls. in late
spring. Edible frs. Size: 10 ×
10ft (3 × 3m). See var.

VALERIANA
Valerian
Valerianaceae
Rhizomatous herbaceous perennial: creeping, mat-forming vars. White/pink/mauve fls. in early summer. Size: up to 5 × 2ft (1.5m × 60cm). See var.

VERBASCUM
Mullein
Scrophulariaceae
Deciduous, semi-evergreen and evergreen shrub, perennial and biennial. Yellow/white/pink/purple fls. in summer. Size: up to 8 × 2½ft (2.5m × 75cm). See var.

VERBENA
Verbenaceae
Perennial and annual (some semi-evergreen). White/pink/red/blue/purple fls. in summer and autumn. Size: up to 5 × 2ft (1.5m × 60cm). See var.

VERONICA
Speedwell
Scrophulariaceae
Herbaceous perennial and sub-shrub, some prostrate, mat-forming vars. White/pink/blue/purple/red fls. from late spring. Size: up to 5 × 2ft (1.5m × 60cm). See var.

VIBURNUM
incl. Snowball, Wayfaring tree, Guelder rose, Withe-rod, Black haw, Cranberry bush
Caprifoliaceae
Deciduous, semi-evergreen and evergreen shrub and tree. For fl. and lf. colour see var. Size: up to 15 × 15ft (4.5 × 4.5m).

VINCA
Periwinkle, Quater, Blue buttons, Trailing myrtle
Apocynaceae
Evergreen trailing sub-shrub and perennial. Pink/blue/mauve/purple/white fls. from spring to autumn. Size: up to 3 × 1½ft (90 × 45cm). See var.

VIOLA
incl. Viola, Violetta, Violet, Pansy, Heartsease, Johnny-jump-up
Violaceae
Deciduous and semi-evergreen sub-shrub, perennial and annual. Fls. all colours, some blotched and bicoloured, all seasons. Size: very small.

VITEX
Chaste tree
Verbenaceae
Deciduous shrub. White/violet fls. in early autumn. Size: 10 × 12ft (3 × 3.5m).

VITIS
Grape vine incl. Amur/Riverbank/Fox/Skunk/Dusty miller/Teinturier grape, Crimson glory flower
Vitaceae
Deciduous perennial climber. Frs. and autumn colour (some vars.). Size: up to 80ft (25m). See var.

WALDSTEINIA
Rosaceae
Evergreen creeping, carpeting sub-shrub. Yellow fls. in spring. Size: very small.

WATSONIA
Bugle lily
Iridaceae
Herbaceous and evergreen corm. White/pink/orange/mauve fls. in summer. Size: up to 5ft (1.5m). See var.

WEIGELA
Caprifoliaceae
Deciduous shrub. Pink/white/red/yellow fls. from late spring. Size: 7 × 6ft (2 × 1.8m).

WISTERIA
Leguminosae
Deciduous perennial woody twining climber. Blue/violet/white/pink fls. in late spring. Size: up to 100ft (30m). See var.

XERANTHEMUM
Everlasting daisy, Immortelle
Compositae
Annual. Purple to white fls. in summer. Size: 3 × 1ft (90 × 30cm).

ZELKOVA
Ulmaceae
Deciduous tree. Autumn colour and frs. Size: at maturity to 100ft (30m).

WULFENIA
Scrophulariaceae
Rhizomatous evergreen rock plant. Violet-blue/pink/white fls. from spring to mid summer acc. to var. Size: very small.

YUCCA
Spanish bayonet/dagger, Adam's needle, Our Lord's candle, Soapweed
Agavaceae
Evergreen shrub and tree. Foliage colour; whitish fls. in late summer. Size: up to 10 × 5ft (3 × 1.5m). See var.

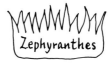

ZENOBIA
Ericaceae
Deciduous or semi-evergreen shrub. White fls. in early summer. Size: 5 × 5ft (1.5 × 1.5m).

XANTHOCERAS
Sapindaceae
Deciduous shrub or small tree. White fls. in spring. Size: up to 20ft (6m).

ZANTEDESCHIA
Arum lily, Calla lily
Araceae
Rhizomatous perennial, some vars. water-loving. Spathe/spadix colours incl. white/yellow/pink/purple fls. from early summer. Size: up to 3 × 2ft (90 × 60cm). See var.

ZEPHYRANTHES
Zephyr/Rain/Atamasco lily, Windflower, Flowers of the west wind
Amaryllidaceae
Bulb. White/pink/yellow fls. from spring to autumn acc. to var. Size: small and very small.

XANTHORHIZA
Incl. Yellowroot
Ranunculaceae
Deciduous shrub. Purple fls. in early spring. Size: 2 × 5ft (60cm × 1.5m).

ZAUSCHNERIA
Californian fuchsia
Onagraceae (sometimes classed in *Oenotheraceae*)
Evergreen, deciduous or herbaceous (depending on climate) sub-shrub. Red fls. from late summer to autumn. Size: small.

ZINNIA
Compositae
Annual. Many colours and multi-coloured fls. in summer. Size: up to 2½ × 1ft (75 × 30cm). See var.

Vegetables and Herbs

ANGELICA
Angelica archangelica
Umbelliferae
Herb.

AUBERGINE
Eggplant
Solanum melongena
Solanaceae
Vegetable/fruit.

BAY *see* SWEET BAY

ANISE
Aniseed
Pimpinella anisum
Umbelliferae
Herb.

AVOCADO
Avocado pear
Persea americana
Lauraceae
Fruit.

BEANS
incl. Broad, French,
   Haricot and Runner
   beans
Phaseolus and *Vicia* spp.
Leguminosae
Pod/seeds.

ARTICHOKE *see* CHINESE
   ARTICHOKE, GLOBE
   ARTICHOKE, JERUSALEM
   ARTICHOKE

BALM
Melissa officinalis
Labiatae
Herb.

BEETROOT
Beta vulgaris
Chenopodiaceae
Root.

ASPARAGUS
Asparagus officinalis
Liliaceae/Asparagaceae
Stalk/shoots.

BASIL
Ocimum basilicum
Labiatae
Herb.

BERGAMOT
Monarda spp.
Labiatae
Herb.

BORAGE
Borago officinalis
Boraginaceae
Herb.

CABBAGE
Brassica oleracea
Cruciferae
Leaf.

CARROT
Daucus carota
Umbelliferae
Root.

BROCCOLI
Calabrese
Brassica oleracea var.
botrytis cymosa
Cruciferae
Flower buds/leaf.

CAMOMILE
Common, garden, Roman,
  Russian camomile
Chamaemelum nobile
Compositae
Perennial herb.

CAULIFLOWER
Brassica oleracea var.
botrytis
Cruciferae
Flower buds/leaf.

BRUSSELS SPROUTS
Brassica oleracea var.
bullata gemmifera
Cruciferae
Leaf.

CARAWAY
Carum carvi
Umbelliferae
Seeds (spice).

CELERIAC
Apium graveolens
Umbelliferae
Root.

BURDOCK
Arctium lappa
Compositae
Root/leaf/stem.

CARDOON
Cynara cardunculus
Compositae
Stalk/shoots.

CELERY
Apium graveolens
Umbelliferae
Stalk/shoots.

CELTUCE
Lactuca sativa var.
angustana
Compositae
Salad.

CHINESE ARTICHOKE
Stachys affinis
Lamiaceae
Tuber.

COMFREY
Borago officinalis
Boraginaceae
Herb.

CHARD
Ruby (rhubarb) Swiss
chard
Beta vulgaris
Chenopodiaceae
Leaf.

CHINESE BROCCOLI
Chinese kale
Brassica alboglabra
Cruciferae
Flower buds/leaf.

CORIANDER
Coriandrum sativum
Umbelliferae
Herb. Seeds/lvs.

CHERVIL
Anthriscus cerefolium
Umbelliferae
Herb.

CHIVES
Allium schoenoprasum
Liliaceae/Alliaceae
Herb.

CORN SALAD
Lamb's lettuce
Valerianella locusta
Valerianaceae
Salad.

CHICORY
Cichorium intybus
Compositae
Salad.

CHOP SUEY GREENS
*Chrysanthemum
coronarium*
Compositae
Salad/leaf.

COURGETTE
Zucchini
Cucurbita pepo
Cucurbitaceae
Vegetable/fruit.

CUCUMBER
Cucumis sativus
Cucurbitaceae
Vegetable/fruit.

ENDIVE
Cichorium endivia
Compositae
Salad.

GLOBE ARTICHOKE
Cynara scolymus
Asteraceae
Stalk/shoots.

DANDELION
Taraxacum officinale
Compositae
Salad.

FENNEL
Foeniculum vulgare
Umbelliferae
Herb and edible bulb acc.
to var.

GOOD KING HENRY
*Chenopodium bonus-
henricus*
Chenopodiaceae
Leaf.

DILL
Anethum graveolens
Umbelliferae
Herb.

FEVERFEW
Tanacetum parthenium
Compositae
Herb.

HAMBURG PARSLEY
*Petroselinum crispum
tuberosum*
Umbelliferae
Root.

EGGPLANT *see* **AUBERGINE**

GARLIC
Allium sativum
Liliaceae/Alliaceae
Bulb.

HORSERADISH
Cochlearia armoracia
Cruciferae
Root.

HYSSOP
Hyssopus officinalis
Labiatae
Herb.

LEEK
Allium ampeloprasum
Liliaceae/Alliaceae
Leaf (base).

MARROW
Cucurbita pepo
Cucurbitaceae
Vegetable/fruit.

JERUSALEM ARTICHOKE
Helianthus tuberosus
Asteraceae
Tuber.

LETTUCE
Lactuca sativa
Compositae
Salad.

MINT
Mentha spicata
Labiatae
Herb.

KALE
Borecole
Brassica oleracea var.
acephala
Cruciferae
Leaf.

LOVAGE
Levisticum officinale
Umbelliferae
Herb.

MIZUNA
Japanese greens
Brassica juncea 'Japonica'
Cruciferae
Salad/leaf.

KOHL RABI
Brassica oleracea
Cruciferae
Root.

MARJORAM
Origanum majorana
Labiatae
Herb.

MUSHROOM
Agaricus bisporus
Fungi
Vegetable/fruit.

NEW ZEALAND SPINACH
Tetragonia expansa
Aizoaceae
Leaf.

PAK CHOI
Brassica chinensis
Cruciferae
Leaf.

PEPPERS
Chillies, incl.
    sweet/Cayenne peppers,
    pimento/pimiento
Capsicum annuum
Solanaceae
Fruit.

OKRA
Hibiscus esculentus
Malvaceae
Pods/seeds.

PARSLEY
Petroselinum crispum
Umbelliferae
Herb.

POTATO
Solanum tuberosum
Solanaceae
Tuber.

ONIONS
incl. Spring onions
Allium cepa
Liliaceae/Alliaceae
Bulb.

PARSNIP
Peucedanum sativum
Umbelliferae
Root.

PUMPKIN
Cucurbita pepo
Cucurbitaceae
Vegetable/fruit.

OREGANO
Origanum majorana
Labiatae
Herb.

PEAS
Pisum sativum
Leguminosae
Pod/seeds.

PURSLANE
Montia sibirica
Portulacaceae
Herb.

RADICCHIO
Cichorium intybus
Compositae
Salad.

 ROSEMARY
Rosmarinus officinalis
Labiatae
Herb.

 SALSIFY
Tragopogon porrifolius
Compositae
Root.

 RADISH
Raphanus sativus
Cruciferae
Root.

 RUE
Ruta
Rutaceae
Herb.

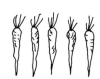 **SAVORY** (winter and
   summer)
Satureia spp.
Labiatae
Herb.

 **RHUBARB**
Rheum rhaponticum
Polygonaceae
Stalk/shoots.

 SAGE
Salvia officinalis
Labiatae
Herb.

 SCORZONERA
Scorzonera hispanica
Compositae
Root.

 ROCKET
Eruca sativa
Cruciferae
Herb.

 SALAD BURNET
Sanguisorba minor
Rosaceae
Salad.

SEAKALE
Crambe maritima
Cruciferae
Stalk/shoots.

SHALLOTS
Allium ascalonicum
Liliaceae/Alliaceae
Bulb.

SQUASH
Cucurbita spp.
Cucurbitaceae
Vegetable/fruit.

SWEET CORN
Maize
Zea mays
Gramineae/Poaceae
Pod/seeds.

SORREL
Rumex acetosa
Polygonaceae
Herb.

SWEDE
Brassica napus
Cruciferae
Root.

TARRAGON
Artemisia dracunculus
Compositae
Herb.

SPINACH
Spinacea oleracea
Chenopodiaceae
Leaf.

SWEET BAY
Laurus nobilis
Lauraceae
Tree/herb.

THYME
Thymus vulgaris
Labiatae
Herb.

SPINACH BEET
Beta vulgaris
Chenopodiaceae
Root.

SWEET CICELY
Myrrhis odorata
Umbelliferae
Herb.

TOMATO
Lycopersicon esculentum
Solanaceae
Vegetable/fruit.

Fruits and Nuts

TURNIP
Brassica campestris
Cruciferae
Root.

ALMOND
Prunus dulcis
Rosaceae
Deciduous nut tree.

BLUEBERRY
Vaccinium corymbosum
Ericaceae
Soft fruit.

WATERCRESS
Nasturtium officinale
Cruciferae
Salad.

APPLE
Malus pumila
Rosaceae
Deciduous fruit tree.

BOYSENBERRY
Rubus
Rosaceae
Soft fruit.

ZUCCHINI *see* COURGETTE

APRICOT
Prunus armeniaca
Rosaceae
Deciduous fruit tree.

CHERRY
Prunus avium
Rosaceae
Deciduous fruit tree.

BLACKBERRY/BRAMBLE
Rubus ulmifolius
Rosaceae
Soft fruit.

CRABAPPLE
Malus
Rosaceae
Deciduous fruit tree.

CURRANTS
Black, red, white currants
Ribes nigrum and
R.sativum
Grossulariaceae
Soft fruit.

GOOSEBERRY
Rubus grossularia
Grossulariaceae
Soft fruit.

LOGANBERRY
Rubus loganobaccus
Rosaceae
Soft fruit.

DAMSON
Prunus damascena
Rosaceae
Deciduous fruit tree.

GRAPE
Vitis vinifera
Vitaceae
Fruiting vine.

MEDLAR
Mespilus germanica
Rosaceae
Deciduous fruit tree.

FIG
Ficus carica
Moraceae
Fruit tree.

GREENGAGE
Prunus italica
Rosaceae
Deciduous fruit tree.

MELON
Cucumis melo
Cucurbitaceae
Fruiting vine.

FILBERT
Corylus maxima
Corylaceae
Deciduous nut tree.

HAZEL COB
Corylus avellana
Corylaceae
Deciduous nut tree.

MULBERRY
Morus nigra and *alba*
Moraceae
Deciduous fruit tree.

NECTARINE
Prunus persica var.
nectarina
Rosaceae
Deciduous fruit tree.

QUINCE
Cydonia oblinga
Rosaceae
Deciduous fruit tree.

WINEBERRY
Rubus phoenicolasius
Rosaceae
Soft fruit.

PEACH
Prunus persica
Rosaceae
Deciduous fruit tree.

RASPBERRY
Rubus idaeus
Rosaceae
Soft fruit.

WORCESTERBERRY
Ribes divaricatum
Grossulariaceae
Soft fruit.

PEAR
Pyrus communis
Rosaceae
Deciduous fruit tree.

STRAWBERRY
Fragaria × ananassa
Rosaceae
Soft fruit.

PLUM
Prunus domestica
Rosaceae
Deciduous fruit tree.

WALNUT
Juglans regia and *nigra*
Juglandaceae
Deciduous nut tree

Paths

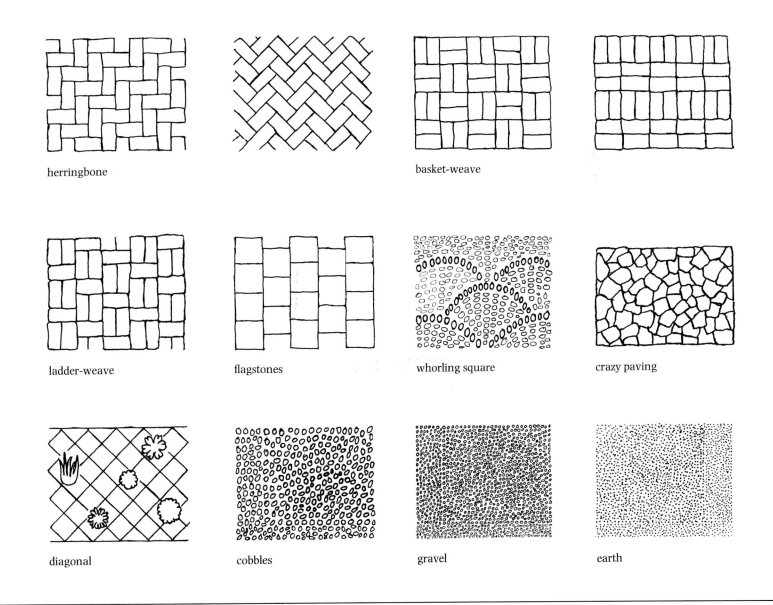

herringbone   basket-weave

ladder-weave   flagstones   whorling square   crazy paving

diagonal   cobbles   gravel   earth

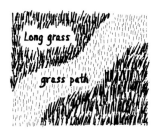

grass path

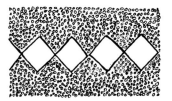

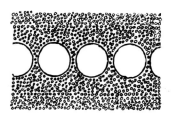

stepping stones through gravel

Edgings

diamond-shaped tiles

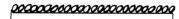

ropework tiles

dogtooth brickwork

curved-top tiles

metal hoops 1

metal hoops 2

pebbles

dwarf box hedge

Topiary and mazes

Water

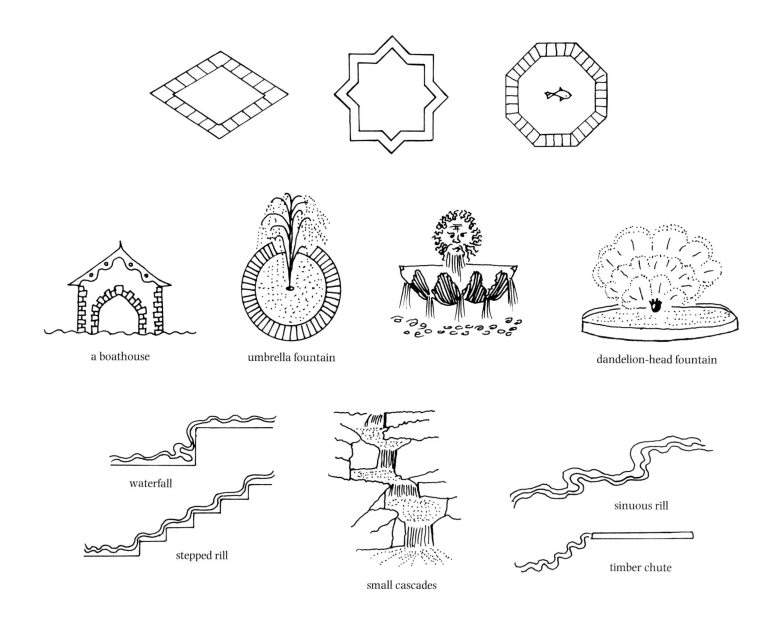

a boathouse

umbrella fountain

dandelion-head fountain

waterfall

stepped rill

small cascades

sinuous rill

timber chute

Summerhouses, greenhouses and sheds

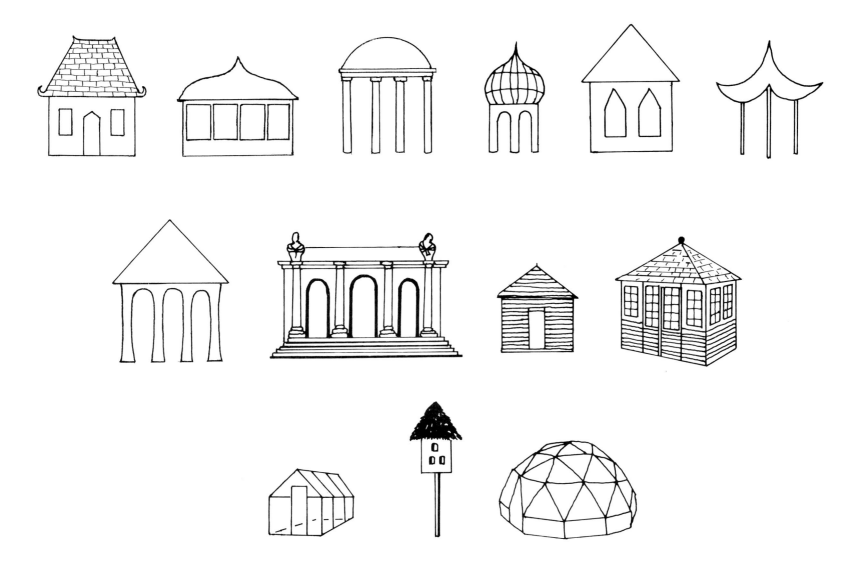

Furniture

Fencing and hedges

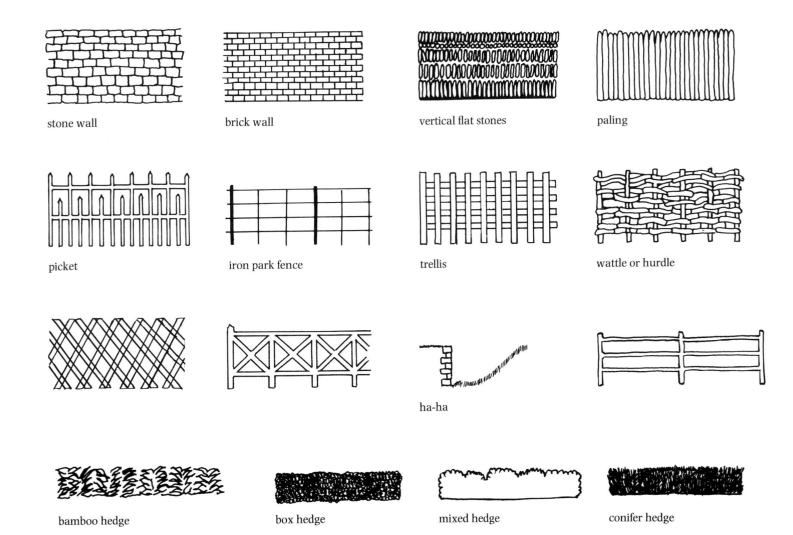

stone wall brick wall vertical flat stones paling

picket iron park fence trellis wattle or hurdle

ha-ha

bamboo hedge box hedge mixed hedge conifer hedge

Gates

Pots and urns

Pruning

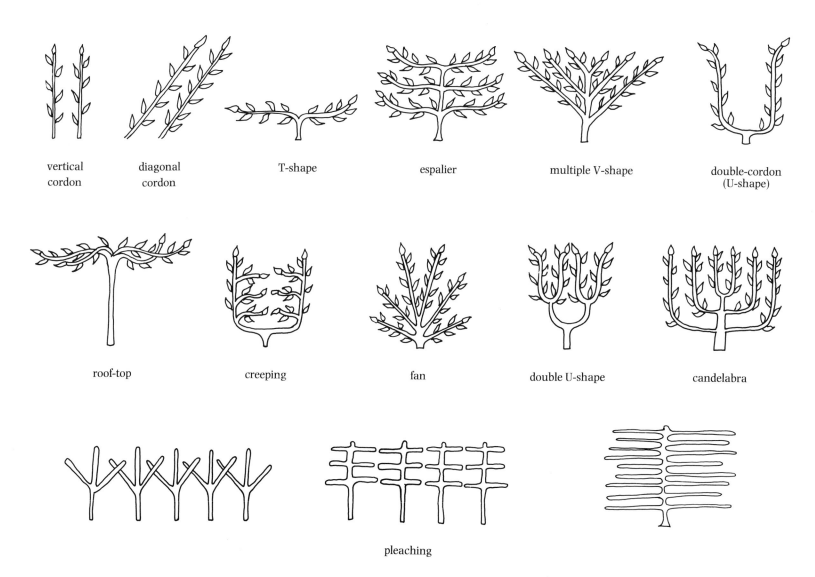

vertical
cordon

diagonal
cordon

T-shape

espalier

multiple V-shape

double-cordon
(U-shape)

roof-top

creeping

fan

double U-shape

candelabra

pleaching

Basic shapes of (a) deciduous and (b) coniferous trees

a

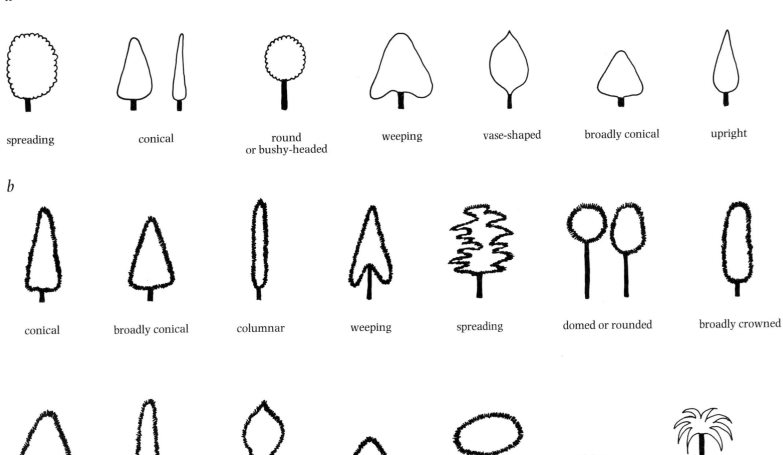

b

spreading	conical	round or bushy-headed	weeping	vase-shaped	broadly conical	upright
conical	broadly conical	columnar	weeping	spreading	domed or rounded	broadly crowned
pyramidal	upright	vase-shaped	globose	rounded crown	prostrate, sprawling or mat-forming	palm

Index of Common Names

Plant symbols in the Dictionary (p. 83) are listed alphabetically under their Latin botanical names. Some English and North American common names are included in the accompanying texts, but only the most familiar common names are listed in this index.

Common name Botanical name

Absinthe *Artemisia*
Acacia *Robinia*
Aconite *Aconitum*
African blue lily *Agapanthus*
African corn lily *Ixia*
African daisy *Osteospermum/ Dimorphotheca*
Alder *Alnus*
Alexandrian laurel *Danäe*
Alkanet *Anchusa*
Almond *Prunus*
Alpine aster *Felicia*
American laurel *Kalmia*
American pawpaw *Asimina*
Andromeda *Pieris*
Angel's fishing rod *Dierama*
Apple *Malus*
Apricot *Prunus*
Arbor-vitae *Thuja/Thujopsis*
Arrowhead *Sagittaria*
Ash *Fraxinus*
Aspen *Populus*
Auricula *Primula*
Australian honeysuckle *Banksia*
Autumn crocus *Colchicum*
Avens *Geum*
Azalea *Rhododendron*

Baboon flower *Babiana*
Baby's breath *Gypsophila*

Baby's tears *Soleirolia*
Bachelor's buttons *Kerria*
Balloon flower *Platycodon*
Balm of Gilead *Populus*
Balsam *Impatiens*
Bamboo *Arundinaria/Phyllostachys/ Pleioblastus/Sasa*
Baneberry *Actaea*
Barberry *Berberis*
Barrenwort *Epimedium*
Basket flower *Centaurea*
Basket of gold *Aucuba*
Bay *Laurus*
Bayberry *Myrica*
Bearberry *Arctostaphylos*
Bear's breeches *Acanthus*
Beauty-berry *Callicarpa*
Beauty-bush *Kolkwitzia*
Bedstraw *Galium*
Beech *Fagus*
Beefsteak plant *Alternanthera/Amaranthus*
Belgian endive *Cichorium*
Belladonna lily *Amaryllis*
Bellflower *Campanula*
Bells of Ireland *Moluccella*
Betony *Stachys*
Bilberry *Vaccinium*
Bindweed *Convolvulus*
Birch *Betula*
Bitter cress *Cardamine*
Bittersweet *Humulus*
Blackberry *Rubus*

Blackberry lily *Belamcanda*
Black-eyed Susan *Thunbergia*
Black gum *Nyssa*
Bladder fern *Cystopteris*
Bladder senna *Colutea*
Bleeding heart *Dicentra*
Blood-flower *Asclepias*
Blood-leaf *Alternanthera*
Bloodroot *Sanguinaria*
Bluebeard *Caryopteris*
Bluebeard lily *Clintonia*
Blueberry *Vaccinium*
Blue-blossom *Ceanothus*
Blue broom *Anthyllis*
Blue button *Amsonia*
Blue cupidone *Catananche*
Blue daisy *Felicia*
Blue dawn flower *Ipomoea*
Blue succory *Catananche*
Bog arum *Calla*
Bog rosemary *Andromeda*
Boneset *Symphytum*
Bonnet bellflower *Codonopsis*
Boston ivy *Parthenocissus*
Bottlebrush *Callistemon*
Boulder fern *Dennstaedtia*
Bouncing Bet *Saponaria*
Bowles's golden grass *Milium*
Box *Buxus*
Bramble *Rubus*
Brass buttons *Cotula*
Bridal wreath *Spiraea*
Bristle club rush *Scirpus*
Brodiaea *Dichelostemma*
Broom *Cytisus*
Brush bush *Eucryphia*
Buckeye *Aesculus*
Buckthorn *Rhamnus*
Bugbane *Cimicifuga*

Bugle *Ajuga*
Bugloss *Anchusa*
Burnet *Sanguisorba*
Burning bush *Kochia*
Bush clover *Lespedeza*
Butcher's broom *Ruscus*
Butterfly bush *Buddleja*
Butterfly flower *Schizanthus*
Butterfly tulip *Calochortus*
Butterfly weed *Asclepias*

California tree poppy *Romneya*
Californian lilac *Ceanothus*
Californian poppy *Eschscholtzia*
Camass *Camassia*
Camomile *Anthemis*
Campion *Lychnis/Silene*
Canary creeper *Tropaeolum*
Candytuft *Iberis*
Canterbury bells *Campanula*
Cape figwort *Phygelius*
Cape leadwort *Plumbago*
Cape marigold *Osteospermum*
Cardinal climber *Ipomoea*
Cardinal flower *Lobelia*
Carnation *Dianthus*
Cassiope *Andromeda*
Castor oil plant *Fatsia/Ricinus*
Catawba *Catalpa*
Cat-tail *Typha*
Cedar *Cedrus*
Celandine *Ranunculus*
Celandine poppy *Stylophorum*
Century plant *Agave*
Chaparral broom *Baccharis*
Cherry *Prunus*
Cherry pie *Heliotropium*
Chestnut *Aesculus/Castanea*